Lecture Notes in Computer Science 10224

Commenced Publication in 1973
Founding and Former Series Editors:
Gerhard Goos, Juris Hartmanis, and Jan van Leeuwen

More information about this series at http://www.springer.com/series/7408

Jürgen Großmann · Michael Felderer
Fredrik Seehusen (Eds.)

Risk Assessment and Risk-Driven Quality Assurance

4th International Workshop, RISK 2016
Held in Conjunction with ICTSS 2016
Graz, Austria, October 18, 2016
Revised Selected Papers

 Springer

Editors
Jürgen Großmann
Fraunhofer FOKUS CC SQC
Berlin
Germany

Michael Felderer
Department of Computer Science
Universität Innsbruck
Innsbruck
Austria

Fredrik Seehusen
SINTEF ICT
Oslo
Norway

ISSN 0302-9743   ISSN 1611-3349   (electronic)
Lecture Notes in Computer Science
ISBN 978-3-319-57857-6   ISBN 978-3-319-57858-3   (eBook)
DOI 10.1007/978-3-319-57858-3

Library of Congress Control Number: 2017938161

LNCS Sublibrary: SL2 – Programming and Software Engineering

Printed on acid-free paper

This Springer imprint is published by Springer Nature
The registered company is Springer International Publishing AG
The registered company address is: Gewerbestrasse 11, 6330 Cham, Switzerland

Preface

Increased connectivity and software complexity lead to an ever-growing demand for techniques to ensure software quality, dependability, reliability, and security. The risks that software systems do not meet their intended level of quality can have a severe impact on vendors, customers, and even society at large. The precise understanding of risks has become one of the cornerstones of critical decision-making within complex social and technical environments.

Traditional approaches for ensuring system quality address risk implicitly rather than systematically. However, there is a growing interest in enhancing traditional approaches for ensuring system quality by taking risk systematically into account. For instance, in traditional test approaches, test planning and prioritization are often based on an implicit notion of risk; systems, functions, or modules, which are known to be critical, are tested more intensively than others. However, taking risk systematically into account allows for a more rigorous prioritization process that is better documented, less dependent on human guesswork, and more easily supported by tools.

The RISK Workshop series has emerged as a high-profile series of events that discusses innovative work in the areas of software risk assessment, testing, and the combination thereof. We have been able to look back on four successful years, in which we have been involved in different conferences and initiated a fruitful exchange between scientists from academia as well as from industry.

This volume contains the proceedings of the 4th International Workshop on Risk Assessment and Risk-Driven Quality Assurance (RISK 2016) held in October 2016 in Graz, Austria, in conjunction with the 28th International Conference on Testing Software and Systems (ICTSS). RISK 2016 brought together researchers from Europe who study, develop, and evaluate innovative techniques, tools, languages, and methods for risk assessment and risk-driven quality engineering. During the workshop, the participants discussed 11 peer-reviewed contributions tackling challenges of assessing and managing safety, security, and reliability risk, and in particular the intersection between these areas. The workshop was structured into three sessions on Security Risk Management, Security Risk Analysis as well as Risk-Based Testing.

We would like to take this opportunity to thank the people who have contributed to the RISK 2016 workshop and helped make it a success. We want to thank all authors and reviewers for their valuable contributions, and we wish them a successful continuation of their work in this area.

March 2017

Jürgen Großmann
Michael Felderer
Fredrik Seehusen

Organization

RISK 2016 was organized by Fraunhofer FOKUS, SINTEF Digital, and the University of Innsbruck.

Organizing Committee

Jürgen Großmann   Fraunhofer FOKUS, Germany
Michael Felderer   University of Innsbruck, Austria
Fredrik Seehusen   SINTEF Digital, Norway

Program Committee

Jürgen Großmann   Fraunhofer FOKUS, Germany
Fredrik Seehusen   SINTEF Digital, Norway
Michael Felderer   University of Innsbruck, Austria
Ina Schieferdecker   TU Berlin/Fraunhofer FOKUS, Germany
Ketil Stølen   SINTEF Digital, Norway
Ruth Breu   University of Innsbruck, Austria
Ron Kenett   KPA Ltd. and University of Turin, Italy
Sardar Muhammad Sulaman Lund University, Sweden
Markus Schacher   KnowGravity Inc., Switzerland
Alessandra Bagnato   Softeam, France
Kenji Taguchi   AIST, Japan
Zhen Ru Dai   University of Applied Science Hamburg, Germany
Per Håkon Meland   SINTEF Digital, Norway
Luca Compagna   SAP Labs, France
Jörn Eichler   Fraunhofer AISEC, Germany
Bruno Legeard   Femto-ST, France
Xiaoying Bai   Tsinghua University, China

Contents

Security Risk Management

Business Driven ICT Risk Management in the Banking Domain with RACOMAT

Johannes Viehmann[✉]

Fraunhofer FOKUS, Berlin, Germany
Johannes.Viehmann@fokus.fraunhofer.de

Abstract. Bringing business risk management and technical security risk management together is one of the major challenges banks currently struggle with in order to increase their resilience against cyber security threats. This short paper presents a systematic approach for such an integrated security risk management which is currently developed in cooperation with a system-relevant bank. The approach uses well known methods and existing standards, it takes advantage of knowledge databases and available generic domain specific models. A first case study has just started. With tool support and especially with a high level of automation the presented approach might become applicable even for large banks.

Keywords: Risk assessment · Security · Business process simulation · Banking

1 Introduction

For banks, managing risks is a vital part of their core business. Whenever they give credit or invest in some business, there is no guarantee that they will get in return what they expect. Banks evaluate both the opportunities and the risks in order to limit their losses and to maximize their profit.

While giving a credit for example has an immanent business risk that the debtor will not be able to repay the loan, there are also operational and technical risks which could cause losses. For example if the credit agreement would be manipulated or lost, that could cause substantial problems. Since today nearly the entire business of banks depends on modern information and communication technology, banks have to defend themselves and their stakeholders especially against cyber security threats.

Eventually in contrast to other organizations in different market sectors, banks are absolutely aware that they have to manage their business risks, their operational and technical risks. Banks do invest significant amounts of money and effort to analyze and treat their security risks, for instance by having redundant backup data centers to prevent that important services become unavailable. Besides their very own interest in doing so, banks are also legally required to manage their risks carefully and to implement certain safeguards.

Since the recent financial crises, even new and stricter international regulations have been initiated in order to prevent future credit- and banking crises, e.g. Basel III [10]. Additionally there are national laws like the German banking act KGW [11].

© Springer International Publishing AG 2017
J. Großmann et al. (Eds.): RISK 2016, LNCS 10224, pp. 3–10, 2017.
DOI: 10.1007/978-3-319-57858-3_1

2   The Problems, Challenges and Related Work

Cooperating with a system-relevant bank in a German BMBF funded research project has revealed that banks do have a strong business risk management and they also have established advanced technical cyber security management capabilities. Nonetheless, it is still challenging for banks to assess the consequences technical issues might have for their core business processes – especially when it comes to indirect, mid-term and long-term consequences. Judging how much banks should invest in their cyber security becomes incredible difficult if little is known about the economic impact.

There are a few academic publications about cyber security risk management in combination with process models, e.g. [12, 13], but they do not specify an applicable way to analyze how exactly technical incidents interact with the business models. In Jakoubi et al. [14] describe concepts to model effects of technical scenarios on business processes. Nonetheless, methods and tools for technical cyber risk management combined with business risk management which are applicable for large organizations like system relevant banks are still not existing.

This short paper shows ongoing research and development efforts to close precisely the gap between business risk management and technical cyber security risk management – especially for the banking domain.

3   Methods and Concepts

Risk management as defined in ISO 31000 [2] includes both risk assessment and risk treatment. Risk assessment means to identify, analyze and evaluate risks while risk treatment tries to reduce risks at least so far that they become acceptable. Risks are events having unwanted consequences. Such incidents in the core banking business processes might directly lead to financial losses for a bank. Unwanted incidents in the ICT typically harm the confidentiality of information, the integrity of data or the availability of services. Costs are not obvious. Before facing the challenges to analyze more indirect consequences and especially to quantify the ICT risks for banks with monetary values, it makes sense to take a look at the basic risk assessment techniques.

There are already lots of established risk assessment methods and concepts that are also suitable for assessing risks in the banking domain. On the technical side, for instance fault tree analysis (FTA) [7], event tree analysis ETA [8], Failure Mode Effect (and Criticality) Analysis FMEA/FMECA [6] or CORAS [1] are popular. The result of the technical risk assessment with any of these methods will be a risk model containing unwanted incidents (events, failures, faults) with some likelihood estimates for their occurrence and information about potential consequences.

For analyzing the consequences, e.g. the CORAS method suggests an asset analysis. After identifying the assets and stakeholders, the effect of the identified incidents can be modeled. This could already build a bridge from the pure technical events to non-technical, economical effects.

But how exactly should it be done? The method suggested in traditional risk assessment methods for the asset analysis is an expert hearing, a workshop. This may be well enough for risk assessment in small organizations. If the task is to assess a large organization having very complicated business processes like a system relevant bank, analysts will eventually get lost without more advanced techniques.

For identifying incidents and for analyzing likelihoods systematically, there are many established concepts and methods that make the analysts life way easier. Using existing risk related databases like check lists for example helps to make sure to cover all already known vulnerabilities, weaknesses and threat scenarios without overlooking any of them. Likelihood values of base incidents like faults or failures are not necessarily only expert estimates or experience values from literature. It is eventually possible to apply objective analytical techniques like security testing for instance and to approximate the observed behavior with likelihood notations. Likelihoods of dependent incidents can be calculated automatically by tools if the dependency relations between the events are modeled correctly.

Similar techniques could help to analyze the business consequences. Leaving the technical level does not mean that systematic objective analysis is not feasible at all.

3.1 Business Simulation Using Models Created with Domain Specific Catalogues

The potential negative economic effects for stakeholders are not limited to loosing assets the stakeholders previously owned. If some of its IT services become unavailable for instance, a bank will neither generate revenue nor profit with these services that do not work properly until they are repaired and fully functional again. So it is not an asset the stakeholders already own that is harmed. Instead the negative economic consequences are lost business opportunities. The bank generates less revenue and less profit.

One idea that comes to mind for analyzing the economic potential under certain conditions is to use event simulations on business process models. Such business simulations could help to study the expected negative effects of unwanted technical incidents. First of all a simulation can be used to assess the opportunities in terms of expected revenue or profit for the case that the IT works perfectly. The expected revenue or benefit in scenarios with temporary disturbances of the involved services can be analyzed in other simulations. This allows analysts to calculate the expected overall financial losses in the simulated time period as the difference between the expected values in the optimal case and in the cases with disturbances.

The business simulations themselves are event simulations and computers can execute them efficiently once they are modeled properly. However, creating appropriate models for the business processes which are detailed enough and contain all dependencies as well as conditions needed to perform correct event simulations is not a trivial task. Also, it must be possible to systematically introduce the immediate effects of technical incidents identified and analyzed in a technical risk assessment into those event simulations at the business level so that realistic behavior can be observed.

To optimally support the task of creating such business models, it makes sense to use existing information and knowledge as far as such information is available. If an organization does not yet have complete high quality models for its core business processes, then eventually some domain specific but otherwise generic models can be used as a starting point.

The BIAN standard [3] offers generic business models for the banking domain. Its exemplary business scenarios are indeed at least a good starting point for analyzing the core business of banks because using the generic BIAN models as a starting point might help to avoid human errors. The BIAN business scenarios are given as sequence diagrams which are very high level and abstract. It is necessary to adapt them carefully to reflect the real world implementations in a specific bank. This task involves some serious effort. It requires excellent knowledge and a certain amount of manual work – but definitely less than starting from scratch. There is an entire BIAN guide for adapting and applying the BIAN standard for a specific bank [9] (Fig. 1).

Fig. 1. Overall risk assessment process

In order to simulate events on the business level, the BIAN sequence diagrams are eventually not detailed enough. For instance, they do not cover session management or rollback behavior if something goes wrong. Modelling processes with more details and behavior for unwanted circumstances as sequence diagrams is probably not the best choice. Sequence diagrams with many alternatives tend to get very confusing. BPMN [4] might be more appropriate to model the more detailed adapted flows.

Additionally, for the assessment of opportunities (and afterwards for the assessment of risks), the business process model must contain information about the economic impact of the process. That requires at least to specify how often the process is executed within a certain time period and how much revenue or profit is generated in the average each time the process is completed successfully. Both the frequency and the average monetary values might change over time. During the night the frequency of banking transactions might be significantly lower, for example. At the end of each month and especially of each year, frequencies might generally be higher. Hence, these values should be specified as functions over the time.

Risk evaluation is only possible for specific stakeholders: One might accept risks others will not take. Therefore, stakeholders should be added to the business model. For each opportunity, it should be specified how big the share for each stakeholder is. Each stakeholder may have his own limits which losses of revenue or profit he would accept. Sometimes the acceptance will be in relation to regular investments and expenses which occur within the same time period. Eventually it makes sense to approximate these regular costs within the same business simulation.

3.2 Modelling the Bridge Between Technical Incidents and Business Processes

In risk assessment, analysts are primarily interested in the cases that something goes wrong. Therefore, it is necessary to add unwanted behavior and failure paths to the business model. In this paper, the focus is on analyzing consequences of technical unwanted incidents in the IT infrastructure of a system relevant bank.

Creating one single large business model that contains also the technical risk assessment would lead to unmanageable complexity. In fact even creating a business model that contains multiple business processes might already be confusing.

Instead, the technical risk assessment and the business risk management should both try to use multiple but small models, only coupled in a loose, flexible way. The basic idea to make it nevertheless possible to analyze all the business consequences is to reproduce just some unwanted technical incidents within multiple high level business event simulations. More precisely the events must be reproduced in the simulation of each business processes that might be affected by the technical incidents. The otherwise independent event simulations on the business level must reflect how the unwanted incidents from the technical risk assessment change business flows.

Of course, therefore it is necessary to somehow connect the various business models with the technical risk assessment artifacts. The BIAN standard describes banking business in a service oriented way with distinct abstract building blocks called Service Domains. Even if banks do not implement everything in a service oriented fashion, this service oriented perspective allows to model isolation levels precisely.

To make it possible to map technical events occurring in some component on Service Domains on which the events might have an effect, it must be modeled how each abstract Service Domain is implemented within the bank. Hence, it is necessary to model, which specific building blocks (e.g. actors, software instances and hardware system) provide the functionality and capabilities the Service Domain describes.

Analyzing the impact of technical incidents will only work if the model reflects where each specific technical building block is used – it can be in many different Service Domains. Having two separate systems does not imply that the incidents on the different systems are statistically independent. If the systems both have installations of the same software program for example, they will have both all the vulnerabilities of that program. Clearly it is important to identify any reused concepts and techniques (i.e. roles, programs, hardware types) as separate specific building blocks.

Using a strict taxonomy for the classification of the specific building blocks and the concept of creating a single bill of materials containing each of these blocks exactly once should help to avoid errors which would lead to models having incorrect dependencies (Fig. 2).

The technical incidents identified and analyzed for the building blocks within each Service Domain must somehow be propagated into the business models of processes using these Service Domains. Looking closer at the nature of the incidents might give a first hint: Most unwanted incidents for IT systems violate confidentiality, integrity or availability. These three categories of technical consequences indicate already how the business risk model could be affected:

In case of reduced availability, dependent business processes will not work as expected. Timeouts might occur and eventually rollbacks have to be performed to keep data consistent. Incoming requests may be rejected. The business simulations can be used to quantify the missed business opportunities with monetary values.

In case of damaged integrity or authenticity, typically assets the stakeholders previously already owned could be harmed as a direct economic consequence.

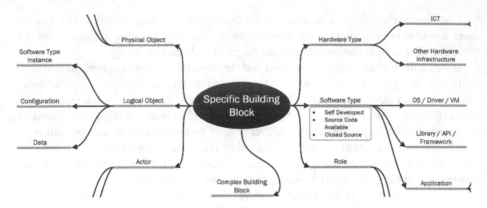

Fig. 2. Excerpt of the taxonomy developed for the bill of materials which are building blocks

In case of lost confidentiality, the most immediate monetary consequences are likely legal consequences: Fines by regulatory bodies and compensation payments for example to customers whose privacy was violated.

Because the banking domain is a highly regulated market sector, significant penalties and compensations might also occur for violated availability or integrity.

In any case, there can be more indirect consequences, especially if the incidents reoccur frequently. Reputation might be damaged and customers could be lost.

3.3 Assessing Legal Risks and Reputation Risks

For analyzing potential legal consequences, business simulations can only help to approximate the expected circumstances of a potential case. Laws and regulations provide eventually ranges for the possible penalties.

An even better source for coming up with numbers for the fines to expect is probably experience from the past – if there have been similar cases and if any experience is already available at all. The fines banks had to pay in a real world cases are a good indicator for how the laws and regulations will actually be applied.

Banking business is all about trust. The reputation that money given to a bank is in good hands, that it is safe, accessible and that it hopefully even generates profit is vital for any bank. If the cyber security of a bank is corrupted, that might cause damage to the reputation. This might make it more difficult to attract new customers and eventually some who are customers will look for another bank to do their business.

To assess changes of the reputation and the monetary effects caused by such changes is more difficult. Besides questioning people, one can try to learn from past incidents, once again. However, it is hard to observe the mid-term and long-term consequences since other factors could overlap and data from other banks will most likely be unavailable.

3.4   Advanced Stakeholder Analysis for Risk Evaluation

Calculating expected losses per time period and comparing these values with the costs stakeholders would eventually accept is a sound approach for the risk evaluation. A simple asset analysis, as it is suggested for example in the CORAS method [1], will not work for a system relevant bank. The complex banking business requires to distinguish between property, opportunities, fines and reputation. Missed opportunities and especially fines in the highly regulated banking domain are for instance the major reason why availability is such a crucial issue for banks. We suggest to do an intense stakeholder analysis that distinguishes carefully between these four categories of consequences. Table 1 summarizes how the technical incidents hint to the consequences and how expected monetary values can be approximated.

Table 1. Artifacts in the advanced consequences and stakeholder analysis

	Property	Opportunity	Legal	Reputation
Caused by technical incidents harming	Integrity	Availability, also integrity	Confidentiality, also availability and integrity	Anything catastrophic or frequently occurring
Methods to approximate monetary values	Expert hearing	Business process simulation	Study fines and compensations e.g. in the past	Question customers, try to learn from history
Difficulty to come up with good numbers	Easy	Moderate	Moderate	Hard
Limit of costs (worst case)	Value of asset	Expenses plus lost potential profit	None	None (because it is long term)

4   Tool Support and Application

While transferring technical incidents into a business risk assessment could eventually be done manually without specialized tools, the event simulations themselves and calculating overall costs will for sure require adequate tool support. The transferring and all modeling might of course benefit from domain specific tool support, too.

RACOMAT [5] is a tool for ISO 31000 conform risk management having built-in support for event simulations. For risk assessment in the banking domain, a domain specific plug-in for RACOMAT has been developed. The plug-in supports the task to adapt and apply models from the BIAN standard, e.g. by creating extended BPMN models preserving the Service Domain structure from the exemplary sequence diagrams semi-automatically. It can extend the model to enable event simulations with default timeout behavior. Taking benefit of CMDB systems, the tool helps to create a catalogue of specific building blocks structured by the building block taxonomy. Modeling relations to Service Domains becomes straight forward with the plug-in.

With the help of the RACOMAT tool and the banking domain specific plug-in, for selected business scenarios and technical incidents, the methods and concepts are currently applied in cooperation with a system relevant bank and a data center provider under realistic conditions as a first case study and as a proof of concept. The first goal is to show that RACOMAT can model and simulate historic cases realistically.

5   Conclusion and Future Work

Due to the complexity of banking business and its massive dependency upon modern ICT, bringing together a technical low level risk management and high level business risk management requires a new systematic approach and tool support. The methods, concepts and tools outlined here may be a step in that direction. That said, more research is required especially to improve scalability.

Some of the ideas presented here are specific for the banking domain, e.g. using BIAN. But it should be possible to develop similar solutions for other domains, using other catalogues of generic business models.

References

1. Lund, M.S., Solhaug, B., Stølen, K.: Model-Driven Risk Analysis – The CORAS Approach. Springer, Heidelberg (2011)
2. International Standards Organization: ISO 31000:2009(E), Risk management – Principles and guidelines (2009)
3. BIAN e.V.: The BIAN Service Landscape Version 4.5, Frankfurt am Main (2016)
4. Tjoa, S.: A formal approach enabling risk-aware business process modeling and simulation. IEEE Trans. Serv. Comput. **4**, 153–166 (2011). doi:10.1109/TSC.2010.17
5. Viehmann, J., Werner, F.: Risk assessment and security testing of large scale networked systems with RACOMAT. In: Seehusen, F., Felderer, M., Großmann, J., Wendland, M.-F. (eds.) RISK 2015. LNCS, vol. 9488, pp. 3–17. Springer, Cham (2015). doi:10.1007/978-3-319-26416-5_1
6. Bouti, A., Kadi, D.A.: A state-of-the-art review of FMEA/FMECA. Int. J. Reliab. Qual. Saf. Eng. **1**, 515–543 (1994)
7. International Electrotechnical Commission: IEC 61025 Fault Tree Analysis (FTA) (1990)
8. International Electrotechnical Commission: IEC 60300-3-9 Dependability management – Part 3: Application guide – Section 9: Risk analysis of technological systems – Event Tree Analysis (ETA) (1995)
9. Rackham, G.: 2015. Banking Industry Architecture Network BIAN - How-to Guide v4: Applying the BIAN Standard, Frankfurt am Main (2016). https://bian.org/assets/bian-standards/bian-service-landscape-4-0/. Accessed 21 Mar 2016
10. Basel Committee on Banking Supervision 2016: Compilation of documents that form the global regulatory framework for capital and liquidity. https://www.bis.org/bcbs/basel3/compilation.htm. Accessed 30 Dec 2016
11. Kreditwesengesetz in der Fassung der Bekanntmachung vom 9. September 1998 (BGBl. I S. 2776), das durch Artikel 5 des Gesetzes vom 23. Dezember 2016 (BGBl. I S. 3171) geändert worden ist. https://www.gesetze-im-internet.de/kredwg/BJNR008810961.html. Accessed 30 Dec 2016
12. Mock, R., Corvo, M.: Risk analysis of information systems by event process chains. Int. J. Crit. Infrastruct. **1**, 247 (2005). doi:10.1504/IJCIS.2005.006121
13. Gjære, E.A., Meland, P.H.: Threats management throughout the software service life-cycle. Electron. Proc. Theor. Comput. Sci. **148**, 1–14 (2014). doi:10.4204/EPTCS.148.1
14. Jakoubi, S., Tjoa, S., Quirchmayr, G.: Rope: a methodology for enabling the risk-aware modelling and simulation of business processes. Presented at the ECIS 2007, AIS (2007)

Towards Transparent Real-Time Privacy Risk Assessment of Intelligent Transport Systems

Gencer Erdogan[✉], Aida Omerovic, Marit K. Natvig, and Isabelle C.R. Tardy

SINTEF Digital, Oslo, Norway
{gencer.erdogan,aida.omerovic,marit.k.natvig,isabelle.tardy}@sintef.no

Abstract. There are many privacy concerns within Intelligent Transport Systems (ITS). On the one hand, end-users are concerned about their privacy risk exposure, while on the other hand, ITS providers need to claim privacy awareness and document compliance with regulations or otherwise face devastating fines. One approach to address these concerns is to use methods specifically developed to assess privacy risks of ITS. The literature lacks such methods, and the complex and dynamic nature of ITS introduces challenges that need to be properly addressed when assessing privacy risks. The main challenges are related to real-time assessment of privacy risks to (1) inform end-users about exposed privacy risks, and (2) help providers asses privacy-compliance risks. We propose a method to privacy risk assessment addressing these challenges. The method is exemplified on an ITS-example. The initial results indicate feasibility of the method and propose directions for future work.

Keywords: Privacy risk assessment · Intelligent Transport Systems · Real-time risk assessment

1 Introduction

Intelligent Transport Systems (ITS) are systems in which information and communication technologies are applied in the field of road transport, including infrastructure, vehicles and users, and in traffic management and mobility management, as well as for interfaces with other modes of transport [2].

There are many privacy risks within ITS solutions due to the wide-spread data recording, exchange of data between systems, and monitoring/tracking of persons and vehicles [7,11]. Much of this data originates from connected persons and connected things associated with persons (e.g. connected vehicles). Thus, ITS may directly or indirectly compromise the identity of persons, their location, plans, and activities. Moreover, service providers in general have to fulfill strict privacy requirements defined by the recent EU Regulation 2016/679 [3], which also requires the citizen's right to a transparent view into the processing of personal data as well as *related privacy risks* (Article 12). Non-compliance with this regulation, which applies from May 2018 will, according to the regulation, result in fines up to 20 million EUR, or in the case of an undertaking,

© Springer International Publishing AG 2017
J. Großmann et al. (Eds.): RISK 2016, LNCS 10224, pp. 11–18, 2017.
DOI: 10.1007/978-3-319-57858-3_2

up to 4% of the total worldwide annual turnover of the preceding financial year [3]. In light of these privacy concerns, there is a need for additional measures to ensure sufficient and adequate safeguards to the user's privacy [11]. One measure is to use methods specifically developed to assess privacy risk of ITS, which are essential for an ITS service provider to be able to claim privacy awareness and to document compliance with regulations.

However, the literature lacks methods specifically to assess privacy risks of ITS, and the complex and dynamic nature of ITS introduces challenges that need to be properly addressed when assessing privacy risks [1]. In this short paper, we first outline needs and challenges within privacy risk assessment of ITS (Sect. 2). Based on this, we describe our initial method in the context of an example (Sect. 3). Finally, we discuss to what extent our current method is feasible with respect to the needs and challenges, before we conclude (Sect. 4).

2   Needs and Challenges

In order to identify needs and challenges within privacy risk assessment of ITS, we conducted an empirical study in terms of identifying state of the art, carrying out a case study on ITS, and carrying out interviews and a workshop together with experts in the field. The empirical study is documented in a publicly available technical report [1]. In this section, we summarize those findings.

In general, end-users make use of ITS services to get assistance in traffic, as well as to plan and carry out journeys. ITS providers, on the other hand, collect data from end-users through ITS services, which monitor and track end-users, to manage the traffic with the main goal to provide better and more useful services. However, very often data is collected, processed, and stored in a manner completely oblivious to the end-user and not in accordance with laws and regulations [8]. Thus, within ITS, end-users are exposed to privacy risks, while ITS providers are exposed to privacy-compliance risks.

Due to the highly dynamic and complex ecosystem of ITS services, end-users need to be informed and be aware of exposed privacy risks in real-time, and based on that decide whether or not to use the service in question.

ITS providers need to obtain a privacy risk picture of their services in real-time, and to properly assess compliance with respect to privacy laws and regulations – in particular compliance with the recent EU Regulation 2016/679 [3].

Privacy risks are in general assessed by making use of general Privacy Impact Assessment (PIA) methods typically based on standards such as ISO 27005, NIST SP 800-30, ISO 29100, and ISO 22307, and are mainly developed and carried out at a governmental level [13]. These methods are often too generic and carried out at a high-level of abstraction, and they need to be specialized towards ITS services. To the best of our knowledge, there are two domain-specific PIA methods for ITS services [4,9]. These approaches are useful for assessing privacy risk of ITS services at business level, but they lack two important features. First, they do not facilitate real-time privacy risk assessment of ITS services. Second, they mainly facilitate privacy risk assessment from the provider point of view, and do not include assessment from the end-user point of view. To summarize, there is need for practically useful computerized methods for real-time privacy assessment of ITS services to:

- Inform end-users about exposed privacy risks caused by ITS services.
- Help ITS providers assess privacy-compliance risks of their services.

3 Initial Method: Example-Driven Feasibility Study

3.1 Method

The main target group of our method is risk managers of ITS providers. Risk assessment is carried out by risk managers to identify, estimate, and evaluate privacy risks end-users may be exposed to. However, end-users and developers are also target groups of the method in the sense that they contribute to the risk assessment by answering a set of questions, and benefit from the assessment results. Risk managers are interested in discovering privacy-compliance risks. End-users are interested in exposed privacy risks caused by ITS services. Developers are interested in privacy risks caused by design decisions.

Our method follows a model-based indicator-driven risk assessment approach. We use the term model in the meaning of graphical/diagrammatic model that captures the privacy risk picture and that supports the calculation of risk-levels based on likelihood and consequence. To this end, we use the CORAS [6] risk modeling language to create privacy risk models. The risk estimation in our method is based on real-time data captured by ITS services, such as the number of times specific parking lots are used, whether electric charging services are in use, the number of times an end-user uses a travel-planning app, etc., as well as information collected from end-users and developers. We collectively refer to such information as indicators and differentiate between three kinds of indicators: real-time ITS indicators (RT), end-user indicators (EU), and developer indicators (D). End-user and developer indicators are obtained through questionnaires answered by end-users and developers, respectively. This information is obtained periodically or on a one-time basis. As illustrated in Fig. 1, the method consists of four steps.

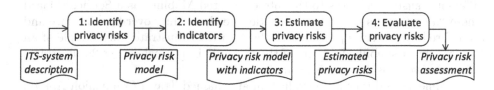

Fig. 1. Method for privacy risk assessment of ITS.

In Step 1, we identify privacy risks by analyzing the target ITS system based on its description with respect to certain privacy assets (e.g. identity of end-users), and develop a model that captures the identified privacy risks. As part of this step we also identify a likelihood scale in terms of frequency intervals, a consequence scale describing the impact by which the privacy of end-user is harmed, and a risk evaluation matrix based on the likelihood and consequence scales (see Fig. 4). We define the likelihood scale as {Rare, Unlikely, Possible, Likely, Certain} and associate each value to a corresponding frequency interval. For example, the likelihood Possible may be defined as frequency interval *[10,50):1w*, which means "from and including 10 to less than 50 times per week." We define the consequence scale as {Insignificant, Minor, Moderate, Major, Catastrophic} and describe each consequence value. The output of this step is a privacy risk model expressed in CORAS [6].

In Step 2, we identify indicators relevant to the risk model. All indicators are defined as questions about a particular fragment of the risk model, and attached to the relevant fragment. The questions are formulated in such a way that the answers are used to support risk estimation (see Fig. 3 for examples). Indicators are categorized either as EU, D, or RT. The output of this step is the same privacy risk model as in Step 1, but now updated with indicators.

In Step 3, we first answer the questions posed by the indicators, and then we use the answers as a basis to estimate the likelihood as well as the consequence of identified privacy risks. The output of this step is the same privacy risk model as in Step 2, but now updated with risk estimates.

In Step 4, we evaluate the identified privacy risks by mapping the risks to the predefined risk matrix with respect to their likelihood and consequence estimates. As illustrated in Fig. 4, risks are grouped in five levels horizontally on the matrix where *Very low* is the lowest risk level and *Very high* is the highest risk level. The risk level is identified by mapping the underlying color to the column on the left-hand side of the matrix. The output of this step is the risk assessment in terms of the matrix including identified risks and their risk level. This output is used by the risk manager to evaluate compliance with privacy-related laws and regulations, provide developers with details about privacy risks at design level (captured by risk models), and inform end-users about exposed privacy risks.

3.2 Applying the Method on an ITS Example Case

Our view of ITS is in line with the envisaged transition from the multitude of different transport services to the interconnected Mobility as a Service (MaaS) where "a customer's major transportation needs are met over one interface and are offered by a service provider" [5,10]. Figure 2a illustrates an example of an ITS system (a simplified version of the example in [1]), while Fig. 2b illustrates a use-case we consider in this example.

Assume an end-user has installed an app named Travel Companion App on the smartphone which enables the user to plan and book multimodal journeys. The user searches on a door-to-door journey using this app. The app sends this request to the MaaS, which in turn requests information from various transport service providers, such as car sharing, public transport etc., in order to construct possible journey routes. Assume now that the MaaS suggests the following journey: (1) take car sharing to the train station, (2) take the train to the city center, (3) take a city bike and bike to your final destination.

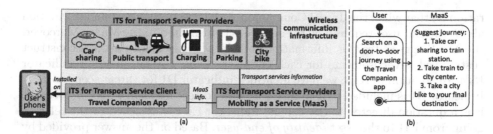

Fig. 2. (a) Simplified example of an ITS system. (b) A use-case in the ITS system.

Step 1. Let us say we are interested in identifying privacy risks with respect to the asset *identity of end-user* (A1). Figure 3 shows a risk model capturing one possible privacy risk UI1 that may compromise the identity of the end-user. This may be caused by a set of threat scenarios (TS1, TS2, TS3, and TS4) initiated by the Travel Companion App (T1). The threat scenarios TS1, TS2, and TS3 are scenarios in which the Travel Companion App shares with the MaaS the end-user's location, age, and exercise habits, respectively. These data may be aggregated by the MaaS and shared with advertisement partners (TS4), which in turn causes the risk UI1. In this example, we define the following likelihood scale {Rare=*[0,5⟩:1w*, Unlikely=*[5,10⟩:1w*, Possible=*[10,20⟩:1w*, Likely=*[20,70⟩:1w*, Certain=*[70,∞⟩:1w*}. For the purpose of the example we only define consequence Major as "personally identifiable information exposed."

Step 2. Figure 3 shows six indicators (gray note-icons) identified for the risk model. Indicators RT1, RT2, RT3, and RT4 are identified for threat scenarios TS1, TS2, TS3, and TS4, respectively. RT1, RT2, and RT3 are based on the

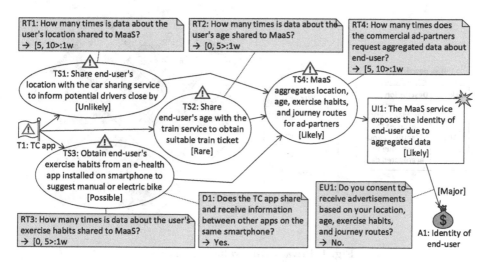

Fig. 3. Privacy risk model for the example use-case in Fig. 2b.

rationale that when the Travel Companion App is used, then certain information about the end-user required by the service is transmitted to the MaaS. Moreover, the MaaS aggregates this information to help advertisement partners construct customized advertisements for each end-user. Thus, the rationale for indicator RT4. In addition to RT3, we have identified indicator D1 for threat scenario TS3. Indicator D1 is included to help assess a more correct frequency for TS3 because it is a question directed to developers. Indicator EU1 is attached to the relation going from UI1 to the asset *identity of end-user*. Based on the answer provided by the end-user for EU1 we may assess the consequence of UI1. This is because some end-users may be willing to provide their identity in order to receive customized advertisements. In that case the consequence of UI1 is reduced.

Step 3. As illustrated in Fig. 3, indicator RT1 returns estimate *[5,10⟩:1w*, which means that threat scenario TS1 occurs with likelihood *Unlikely* according to the predefined likelihood scale. Similarly, we see that the likelihood of TS2 is *Rare* based on indicator RT2. TS3, however, is estimated to likelihood *Possible*. This is because the answer to indicator D1 is *Yes*, and based on this we choose to increase the likelihood from *Rare* (in the case where only RT3 is considered for TS3) to likelihood *Possible*. Assuming TS1, TS2, and TS3 are separate, we find out the likelihood of TS4 by adding the likelihoods of TS1, TS2, and TS3 [6], which gives *[15,35⟩:1w*. We also need to add the frequency provided by RT4. This results in frequency *[20,45⟩:1w*, which means that TS4 occurs with likelihood *Likely*. Thus, UI1 has likelihood *Likely*. The answer to indicator EU1 is *No*. Based on this, we choose to estimate the consequence of UI1 as *Major*.

Step 4. Based on Step 3, we see that the privacy-risk UI1 occurs with likelihood *Likely*, and has a *Major* consequence on asset *identity of end-user*. We map this to the risk matrix and see that UI1 has risk level *High* (see Fig. 4).

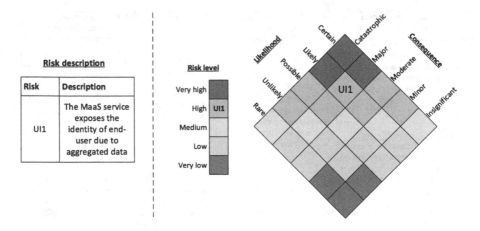

Fig. 4. Privacy risk evaluation matrix.

4   Discussion and Conclusion

In this section, we first discuss to what extent our method is feasible w.r.t. the needs and challenges pointed out in Sect. 2, before we conclude.

Inform end-users about exposed privacy risks caused by ITS services. The risk evaluation matrix (Fig. 4) is the final output of our method and is provided to the end-user. The matrix contains the identified privacy risks, their likelihood, their consequence, as well as their risk level. The risk descriptions provide an explanation to the end-user about the exposed privacy risks. The likelihood and consequence scales on the matrix show the end-user the likelihood and consequence for each exposed privacy risk. The risk-level column provides the risk level of each identified risk plotted in the matrix. Based on this information the end-user is informed about exposed privacy risks as well as their risk level in a transparent manner. This is transparent in the sense that the risk assessment is carried out by the ITS service provider and made available to the end-user. We do not describe the risk levels because the risk acceptance criteria may vary among end-users. Finally, the EU indicators not only support the risk assessment, but also inform the end-user about user-specific information taken into account in the risk assessment.

Help ITS providers assess privacy-compliance risks of their services. Our method is mainly developed to carry out risk assessment on behalf of end-users with respect to privacy-related assets important to end-users, such as identity (example in Sect. 3.2). Laws and regulations such as the EU Regulation 2016/679 [3] mainly consist of requirements specifically focused on the privacy of end-users that providers must fulfill. Thus, to this end, our approach is useful for assessing privacy-compliance risks that address requirements focused on the privacy of end-users. Moreover, the usage of indicators in the risk models helps the ITS providers to link risks to privacy-specific laws and regulations in one model.

Real-time privacy risk assessment. Our current (initial) approach is supported by the necessary foundation for tool support and automation. CORAS [6] is supported by formal rules to calculate risks, and we may use existing guidelines [12] to schematically translate CORAS risk models into executable algorithms. Based on input provided by the indicators, the algorithms may assess the privacy risks captured by the risk models. We are confident that this envisioned solution for tool-support is feasible as we have in fact taken part in implementing a similar approach in a framework for real-time cyber-risk assessment developed by the WISER-project [12]. However, although indicator-driven real-time assessment do exist within cybersecurity [12], this is yet an unexplored area within the domain of privacy assessment of ITS [1], and as future work we plan to investigate how real-time information may be obtained from ITS to support privacy risk assessment.

In conclusion, there is need for practically useful support for real-time privacy assessment of ITS services to (1) inform end-users about exposed privacy risks caused by ITS services, and (2) help ITS providers assess privacy-compliance risks of their services. In this short paper, we provide an initial method for a transparent real-time privacy risk assessment of ITS addressing the aforementioned needs. The innovative contribution of the paper is integration of indicators in the privacy assessment. If valid and reliable, the indicators are expected to facilitate the capturing of relevant changes in privacy issues so that end-users and ITS providers can timely be informed. We currently claim that the approach is ITS-specific since we so far have only evaluated it on the ITS domain. Generality of the approach will depend on results of future evaluations on other domains. The evaluation so far indicates that our approach is one step at the right direction. A natural part of further evaluation would be to assess the effectiveness of our approach w.r.t. needs of the stakeholders.

Acknowledgments. This work has been conducted as part of the PrivacyAssessment@SmartCity project funded by SINTEF, as well as the WISER project (653321) funded by the European Commission within the Horizon 2020 research and innovation programme.

References

1. Erdogan, G., Omerovic, A., Natvig, M.K., Tardy, I.C.R.: Needs and challenges concerning privacy risk management within Intelligent Transport Systems. Technical report A27830, SINTEF (2016)
2. European Parliament. Directive 2010/40/EU (2010)
3. European Parliament. Regulation (EU) 2016/679 (2016)
4. Friginal, J., Guiochet, J., Killijian, M.-O.: Towards a privacy risk assessment methodology for location-based systems. In: Stojmenovic, I., Cheng, Z., Guo, S. (eds.) MindCare 2014. LNICSSITE, vol. 131, pp. 748–753. Springer, Cham (2014). doi:10.1007/978-3-319-11569-6_65
5. Hietanen, S.: MaaS-the new transport model? Eurotransport Mag. **12**(2), 2–4 (2014)
6. Lund, M.S., Solhaug, B., Stølen, K.: Analysis, Model-Driven Risk: The CORAS Approach. Springer, Heidelberg (2011)
7. Psaraki, V., Pagoni, I., Schafer, A.: Techno-economic assessment of the potential of intelligent transport systems to reduce CO2 emissions. IET Intel. Transport Syst. **6**(4), 355–363 (2012)
8. Pultier, A., Harrand, N., Brandtzæg, P.B.: Privacy in mobile apps: measuring privacy risks in mobile apps. Technical report A27493, SINTEF (2016)
9. Ren, D., Du, S., Zhu, H.: A novel attack tree based risk assessment approach for location privacy preservation in the VANETs. In: Proceedings of IEEE International Conference on Communications (ICC 2011), pp. 1–5. IEEE (2011)
10. Spickermann, A., Grienitz, V., von der Gracht, H.A.: Heading towards a multi-modal city of the future? Multi-stakeholder scenarios for urban mobility. Technol. Forecast. Soc. Chang. **89**, 201–221 (2014)
11. Vandezande, N., Janssen, K.: The ITS directive: more than a timeframe with privacy concerns and a means for access to public data for digital road maps? Comput. Law Secur. Rev. **28**(4), 416–428 (2012)
12. WISER: Cyber risk modelling language and guidelines, preliminary version. Technical report D3.2, WISER (2016)
13. Wright, D., de Hert, P.: Privacy Impact Assessment. Springer, Heidelberg (2012)

Check Your Blind Spot: A New Cyber-Security Metric for Measuring Incident Response Readiness

Benjamin Aziz[1(✉)], Ali Malik[1], and Jeyong Jung[2]

[1] School of Computing, University of Portsmouth, Portsmouth, UK
{benjamin.aziz,ali.al-bdairi}@port.ac.uk
[2] Institute of Criminal Justice Studies, University of Portsmouth, Portsmouth, UK
jeyongj@gmail.com

Abstract. This paper presents some ideas on defining and implementing a new Cyber-security risk metric for measuring the readiness of organisations, in terms of the availability of their resources, in dealing with new attack incidents launched against their infrastructures whilst recovering from ongoing incidents. Our new metric, the Mean Blind Spot, is defined as the average interval between the recovery time of an existing incident and the occurrence time of a new incident. It is therefore designed to capture those time intervals where the organisation is most vulnerable due to possible lack of available resources. We present an approach for implementing our new metric using open data on security incidents available from the VERIS community dataset.

1 Introduction

In the context of computing and Cyber systems, measuring risk means choosing an aspect of vulnerability that may exist in a system to investigate, such as its resistance to threats or its exposure to attack incidents. The unit by which risk is measured is usually called the *risk metric*. For example, to measure the frequency at which security attacks occur in some system, one may adopt a risk metric that represents the mean time across these occurrences. Using metrics is a good method for both the quantification of IT risks and reflection of business needs [10]. They are used as objective grounds when an organisation needs to make a decision on its strategy or resource distribution in relation to its IT infrastructure.

Cyber-security risk metrics provide an insight for organisations into the resilience of their IT infrastructure against attacks carried out from over the Internet. As a result, they also give an indication of the cost that may be incurred from the aftermath recovery of such attacks and the cost needed in the future to defend against them. In literature, there have been several efforts that attempt to define and collect such Cyber security-related metrics, examples of which include [4,7,11]. And despite recent surveys (e.g. [12]) that question the validity and usefulness of quantified security, we agree more with the view by [3] that

© Springer International Publishing AG 2017
J. Großmann et al. (Eds.): RISK 2016, LNCS 10224, pp. 19–33, 2017.
DOI: 10.1007/978-3-319-57858-3_3

past data are still relevant to new security incidents and that despite the fact that *the road ahead may bend with human whim and technological advance, ... it does not appear to bend too sharply too often.* Therefore having some idea of the quantitative aspects of security is better than none.

We introduce in this paper a new Cyber-security metric, which we term the *Mean Blind Spot* metric. The new metric is based on the concept of a *blind spot*, which represents the time interval between the moment of occurrence of a new security incident and the moment at which an existing incident has been fully recovered. As such, a blind spot reflects the notion of *readiness* of an organisation or its IT security team to deal with new security incidents as they occur while dealing with the recovery from existing ones. Such readiness assumes that the deployment of resources to the recovery of incidents can only contribute positively to that recovery. Although our new metric does not identify the cause of a problem nor suggest a solution for the cause, it can work as objective evidence when an IT manager argues for more organisational support or resources to secure their infrastructure. We define an implementation of this metric in an open-source community dataset.

The rest of the paper is structured as follows. In the next Sect. 2, we review related work including the collection of Cyber-security and network security risk metrics defined in [4,7,11]. In Sect. 3, we give a quick background on a couple of closely related Cyber-security metrics and demonstrate their definitions with a simple running example. In Sect. 4, we introduce our new metric, the Blind Spot, and discuss its rationale and definition, including some variations that represent higher-level views of the problem of blind spots. In Sect. 5, we present our implementation using the VERIS dataset. Finally, in Sect. 6, we conclude the paper and give directions for future work.

2 Related Work

As the dependence on ICTs of an organisation increases, it is important that information security is integrated into business strategies. Many studies [5,6,9] suggest that senior management should discuss IT agendas and issues as business matters. However, top decision-makers are not familiar with IT terms but with business language. If information security issues are not explained in business terms, it may be hard to gain support from senior managers. Generally, there needs to be two things in place to aid the understanding of senior managers. The first is the quantification of IT issues and responsive measures. When security risks and countermeasures are quantified, it becomes much easier to calculate business impact resulting from IT issues. The second relates IT issues to business goals and objectives, where IT agendas reflect needs of businesses [5].

Many attempts have been made to suggest standardised Cyber-security metrics for organisations. Each study has a different approach. As an international body of the UN, the Telecommunication Standardisation sector of the International Telecommunication Union (ITU-T) published Cyber-security indicators of risk [11], which included not only technical factors but also human factors as well. Indicators such as "security training and education" and "personnel security" were adopted to reduce human errors or intended behaviours in an organisation.

On the other hand, the Center for Internet Security (CIS) metrics [4] focus mostly on technical and business factors without consideration of human factors. The CIS defined in [4] seven metrics that are directly related to the overall incident management process, ranging from incident detection to incident recovery. We adopt two such technical metrics defined in [4] as the basis for our work here.

Criticising past metrics as "labour intensive" and "subjective", Lippman et al. [7] argued that continuous risk assessment based on a data-driven approach was necessary to reflect the constantly changing nature of threats. The metrics proposed in [7] are of complex mathematical nature and hence their applicability is questionable. Chew et al. [2] suggest three types of metrics used differently depending on the purpose and nature of a metric. Implementation metrics are intended to measure the extent at which security policies are implemented. Secondly, effectiveness/efficiency metrics measure how well security services are delivered. Lastly, impact metrics aim to measure impacts of security incidents on a business.

One could argue that the work presented here involves the second type of metrics, since the aim of the work is to define metrics that measure the readiness of an IT department within an organisation when facing incidents over time. Measuring the readiness of security services allows for the diagnoses of an organisation on its capability of handling unexpected incidents.

Payne [8] suggested seven key steps to establishing a security metrics programme. One of them is to establish benchmarks and targets. Setting benchmarks is useful when evaluating success or failure of current security controls [1]. There should be some criteria for benchmarks. Too simplistic metrics may not be appropriate for being regarded as benchmarks because they are naturally intuitive or self-explanatory. Thus, creating an advanced metric based on basic ones is a good practice that we adopt in our approach. Also, metrics for benchmarks need to be used for driving improvements for existing practices. It means that they have actual impact on IT or business management.

In our case, we adopt a widely used large community dataset called VERIS [13] as our benchmark on which we implement our new incident readiness metrics. After a benchmark is adopted in an organisation, there is no hard and fast rule as to choosing a reference point for the benchmark. The choice of acceptable levels for our metrics will depend on organisational context.

3   Background

Literature has numerous metrics related to Cyber security (e.g. [4,7,11]). We give here an overview of two such closely related metrics defined in [4], which we use later as part of the definition of our new set of metrics. We also give an overview of a widely-used security incident vocabulary and dataset known as VERIS, which we use as a benchmark reference for the implementation of our new metrics.

3.1 Mean Time Between Security Incidents

The Mean Time between Security Incidents (MTBSI) metric is described in [4] as a metric for calculating the mean time between occurrences of security incidents in some organisation's IT infrastructure. This type of operational metrics can be defined by the following formula:

$$MTBSI = (\sum_{i=1}^{n-1}(Date\_of\_Occurence(incident_{i+1})-$$

$$Date\_of\_Occurence(incident_i)))/(n-1) \qquad (1)$$

where n is the total number of recorded incidents. As a result, there would be only $n-1$ intervals between any n incidents. We consider the unit of measurement of the MTBSI metric to be time, e.g. hours, days, weeks etc. The following Table 1 shows an example of 10 incidents recorded with the dates and times of their occurrences.

Table 1. An example of incident occurrence dates and times

Incident number	1	2	3	4	5
Date of occurrence	01.06	01.06	01.06	01.06	01.06
Time of occurrence	12:10	12:50	14:00	14:56	18:30
Incident number	6	7	8	9	10
Date of occurrence	01.06	02.06	02.06	02.06	02.06
Time of occurrence	18:35	07:20	09:20	12:30	19:40

To calculate the MTBSI for this example, we evaluate Eq. (1) above:

$$MTBSI = \frac{(40+70+56+214+5+765+120+190+430)}{9} = 210 \text{ min.}$$

This means that, on average, there are 3.5 h separating the occurrence of any two incidents.

3.2 Mean Time to Incident Recovery

The second widely-used metric for measuring Cyber security is the Mean Time to Incident Recovery (MTIR), which reflects the mean time needed from the moment an incident occurs to the moment it is recovered.

This type of operational metrics can be defined using the following formula from [4]:

$$MTIR = (\sum_{i=1}^{n}(Date\_of\_Recovery(incident_i)-$$

$$Date\_of\_Occurence(incident_i)))/n \qquad (2)$$

where n is the total number of recorded incidents. We take the unit of measurement for MTIR again to be time, e.g. hours, days, weeks etc. Note that we divide over n since the number of recoveries is the same as the number of incidents occurring. For example, in the following Table 2, we have again the same 10 incidents recorded from Table 1, but this time also with their dates and times of recovery.

Table 2. An example of incident occurrence/recovery dates and times

Incident number	1	2	3	4	5	6	7	8	9	10
Date of occurrence	01.06	01.06	01.06	01.06	01.06	01.06	02.06	02.06	02.06	02.06
Time of occurrence	12:10	12:50	14:00	14:56	18:30	18:35	07:20	09:20	12:30	19:40
Date of recovery	01.06	01.06	01.06	01.06	01.06	01.06	02.06	02.06	02.06	03.06
Time of recovery	13:55	14:40	19:30	19:05	20:10	21:30	11:10	13:50	15:50	00:15

To calculate MTIR for this example, we evaluate Eq. (2) above:

$$MTIR = \frac{(105+110+330+249+100+175+230+270+200+275)}{10} = 204.4 \text{ min.}$$

This means that each incident takes on average about 3 h and 24 min to recover.

3.3 VERIS

The Vocabulary for Event Recording and Incident Sharing (VERIS) [13] is a dataset and schema capturing a set of metrics for describing security incidents. It is currently considered a leading provider of open quality information in the IT security domain and provides a framework that organisations can use to collect and share information on security incidents in a responsible and anonymous manner, with the aim of constructing a ground on which researchers and experts in the IT security industry can cooperate to learn from their experiences. We use the dataset provided in VERIS, known as VCDB [14], as a benchmark on which we implement our new blind spot-based metrics defined in the next sections.

The VERIS schema itself consists of five general sections, containing descriptions of the security incidents in the VERIS dataset. These five categories are as follows:

- *Incident Tracking*: this section contains general information about the incidents, for example, the source identity, summary of the incident and whether the incident is related to other incidents.
- *Victim demographies*: this section contains information related to the organisation being affected by the incident, for example, its country of operation, number of employees, revenue and industry type.
- *Incident description*: this section contains information related to the question of "who did what to what (or whom) with what result".

- *Discovery and response*: this section contains information related to the incident's timeline, its discovery method, root causes, corrective actions etc.
- *Impact assessment*: this last section contains information on loss categorisation and estimation, impact rating and so on.

For the purpose of this paper, we are mainly interested in one kind of information; namely *time to containment*. This is the closest in nature to the MTIR metric described above, and appears under the "Discovery and response" section of information. In VCDB, this metadata appears as *timeline.containment*. The available meaningful values for the timeline unit for this metadata include seconds, minutes, hours, days, weeks, months, years and never. Other values are NA and unknown, but we do not consider these to be useful.

The significance of the VERIS dataset lies in the fact that it is a *community-based* dataset. This means that its data are collected from a wide range of industries and varied over different types and sizes of organisations. This renders it more interesting and with wider applicability than datasets generated in single organisations.

4 The Mean Blind Spot Metric

Our new incident readiness metrics rely on a concept we call the *Blind Spot* (BS). A BS is the time interval between the moment a new security incident occurs and the last moment the previous security incident was recovered, as shown in Fig. 1. In its worse case, a BS represents the time when an organisation has to start recovery from a new incident whilst still recovering from an earlier one. We consider this metric to be an indication to the readiness of an organisation to encounter new incidents and a measure of the vulnerability organisations may face in such situations where not enough resources are available to recover from security incidents.

Note at this stage that, for the sake of simplicity, we do not consider part of this model the scenario when two incidents arrive exactly at the same moment in

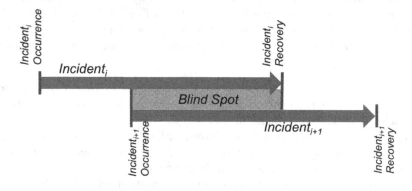

Fig. 1. A Blind Spot

time (i.e. when $Date\_of\_Occurence(incident_i) = Date\_of\_Occurence(incident_{i+1})$).
This is justified since later during the VERIS-based implementation part, we
replace this difference in arrival time with the MTBSI metric (and again assume
that MTBSI > 0).

We can average out this difference in occurrence times of new incidents and
the recovery times of older ones in terms of the *Mean Blind Spot* (MBS) metric
as follows:

$$MBS = (\sum_{i=1}^{n-1}(Date\_of\_Occurrence(incident_{i+1}) -$$
$$Date\_of\_Recovery(incident_i)))/(n-1) \qquad (3)$$

The unit of measurement for the MBS metric is time, e.g. hours, days, weeks
etc. The mean is calculated over $n-1$, as there are only $n-1$ blind spots for n
number of recorded incidents, as shown in Fig. 2.

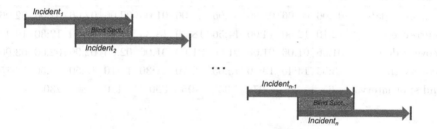

Fig. 2. $n-1$ Chain of Blind Spots

There are a couple of important assumptions this definition relies on:

- The definition assumes a *first-come-first-serve* model of scheduling incidents
  to recovery resources, or in other words, incident i is scheduled for recovery
  before incident $i+1$. This is important for the blind spot time area to be
  a true one, otherwise it will contain the idle time that an incident spends
  waiting in the scheduling queue.
- The second assumption relies on the fact that all the recovery resources will
  contribute positively to all the occurring security incidents. In reality, this
  may not always be the case. Some resources may require some time to become
  positive contributors to the reduction of the recovery time for an incident. In
  fact, some resources may only have negative contribution to the recovery of
  an incident. This situation is depicted in Fig. 3, where we only assume Type
  1 resources in our model.

Let's consider how the MBS metric works through an example. The following
Table 3 shows again our 10 security incidents with their occurrence and recovery
times, but this including also their blind spot times.

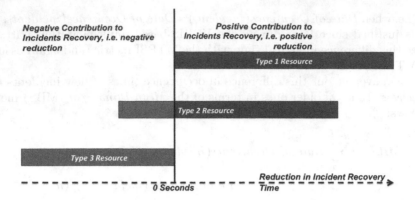

Fig. 3. Resources Contribution to Incident Recovery

Table 3. An example showing blind spots

Incident number	1	2	3	4	5	6	7	8	9	10
Occurrence date	01.06	01.06	01.06	01.06	01.06	01.06	02.06	02.06	02.06	02.06
Occurrence time	12:10	12:50	14:00	14:56	18:30	18:35	07:20	09:20	12:30	19:40
Recovery date	01.06	01.06	01.06	01.06	01.06	01.06	02.06	02.06	02.06	03.06
Recovery time	13:55	14:40	19:30	19:05	20:10	21:30	11:10	13:50	15:50	00:15
Blind spot interval	−65	−40	−274	−35	−95	590	−110	−80	230	-

Note that for the last incident, there is no blind spot time as no incidents are recorded after that. For this example, we can calculate MBS as follows:

$$MBS = (((-65) + (-40) + (-274) + (-35) + (-95) + 590 + (-110) + \\ (-80) + 230))/9 = 13.44 \text{ min.}$$

A positive value (as in this case) for the MBS metric is good, since it indicates that there is a positive time margin between, on average, the occurrence and recovery of incidents. However, a negative value would signal no such margin exists and that incidents' recovery stages are overlapping. This may further have implications on an organisation's capability to cope with the speed of occurrence of security incidents since recovery from earlier incidents is, on average, slow.

We next discuss one variant of this metric, which incorporates an organisation's appetite for blind spots.

4.1   An Approximated MBS

A first variation of the MBS metric that we introduce is an approximated one, which can be calculated directly using the MTIR and MTBSI metrics discussed earlier. We call this variation the Approximate MBS (AMBS) metric. The general formula for the AMBS metric is as follows:

$$AMBS = \frac{MTIR}{MTBSI} \tag{4}$$

The intuition behind this metric is that it gives some sense of how large the difference is between recovery and incident occurrence intervals as captured by the MTIR and MTBSI metrics, respectively. Therefore, it provides a quick way of understanding the effect of the blind spot problem. If, on average, recovery intervals are smaller than incident occurrence intervals, then this ratio would be less than one, which is good for the organisation. If, on the other hand, the ratio is one or more, it means that the occurrence intervals are at least as large as the recovery ones, on average, which is bad for the organisation.

Consider again the example of the previous section. We calculated that MTIR = 204.4 min/interval and that MTBSI = 210. Therefore, one can calculate AMBS = 204.4/210 = 0.973. This value, enforces the conclusion arrived at by the calculation of the MBS metric that on average, in the case of our example, blind spots do not pose a problem in terms of overall time they last. As we see later in Sect. 5, this metric also gives an indication as to the maximum number of incidents an organisation may be recovering from in any one moment in time.

4.2 Ratio of Blind Spots Metric

The Ratio of Blind Spots (RBS) metric is not, strictly speaking, based on the MBS metric but more fundamentally based on the concept of a blind spot. In order to define RBS, we first define a Blind Spot Appetite (BSA) value, which represents the maximum blind spot time an organisation or an IT team is willing to tolerate. For example, a BSA value might be −60 min, meaning that the organisation is willing to tolerate scenarios where recovery from an existing incident overlaps the occurrence of a new one in a maximum of one hour.

The ratio BS/BSA therefore represents a measure of how far a blind spot is from the appetite value. A value of BS/BSA = 1 or less means that the blind spot is within the acceptable range and a value of more than 1 means that the blind spot is unacceptable. For simplicity, we approximate all the values of BS/BSA < 0 to 0, since in this case these have the same meaning as to when BS/BSA = 0. Returning to the example of the previous section, we calculate the BS/BSA values for each blind spot as shown in Table 4.

Based on the BS/BSA ratio, one can define the new RBS metric as follows, in terms of the cardinality of a multiset (bag) of all those ratios who's value is over 1:

Table 4. Example showing the ratio BS/BSA

Incident number	1	2	3	4	5	6	7	8	9	10
Blind Spot interval	−65	−40	−274	−35	−95	590	−110	−80	230	
BS/BSA ratio	1.08	0.67	4.57	0.58	1.58	0	1.83	1.33	0	

$$RBS = \frac{card(\{|y \; where \; (y = BS/BSA) \; \wedge \; (y > 1)|\})}{n-1} \times 100\% \qquad (5)$$

The RBS metric hence captures the percentage of the ratio of all the BS/BSA elements, which are over 1, over the overall number of blind spots. Unlike MBS, it does not rely on a mean-based calculation, but represents more the percentage of "risky" blind spots in an organisation or an IT team. In our example, RBS = $card(\{1.08, 4.57, 1.58, 1.83, 1.33\})/9 \times 100\% = 56\%$. This means that, despite the fact that MBS is on average positive, 56% of blind spots are risky.

5   Method Implementation Using VERIS

In this section, we propose a practical approach for implementing our new metrics using the VERIS dataset (VCDB) [14]. This implementation will allow organisations to obtain some idea of their level of readiness in dealing with blind spots, without the need for much precise information about their own security incidents.

5.1   Implementing the MBS Metric

Our first implementation provides a measurement function for new organisations to assess their level of readiness based on two pieces of information: First their MTBSI metric values and second the time to containment metric in the VERIS dataset. Note that here we parameterise by MTBSI since VERIS, despite its rich collection of incident metadata, does not specify whether two incidents belong to the same organisation and in what temporal order they occur.

We define the signature of the blind spot readiness measurement function, f, as follows:

$$f : Time \rightarrow Percentage \qquad (6)$$

which takes in a time unit expressing the MTBSI for the particular organisation, and returns a percentage number expressing the level of blind spot readiness for that organisation. This is the compliment of the percentage of incidents that are deemed to be *risky* with respect to the information provided by the VERIS dataset, in the sense that there is high likelihood that the organisation may not be prepared to contain them in good time.

Our definition of f is constrained by two aspects of the VERIS dataset: First, there are no timeline information across the reported incidents, which means that it is not possible to conclude, given two incidents, what their sequence is. Second, no concrete timeline data is given; only time units (e.g. hours, days, weeks, etc.) As a result, our implementation relies on the relationship between the lengths of the MTIR (i.e. time to containment) and MTBSI metrics when deciding whether a blind spot exists or not.

Figure 4 depicts the relationship between a blind spot and the MTIR and MTBSI metrics. In the absence of concrete dates/times marking the start and

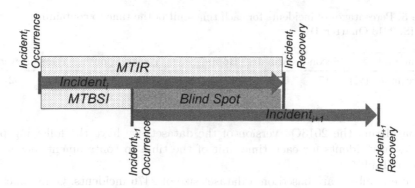

Fig. 4. Relationship between a Blind Spot and MTIR, MTBSI

recovery points of incidents, we consider MTBSI as the metric describing the uniform time difference between consecutive incident occurrences, and MTIR as the metric describing the uniform time between the start and recovery times of incidents. As a result, an MTIR value that extends beyond MTBSI is in a blind spot area, and one that does not is not. As a consequence of the lack of precise information on incident occurrence and recovery times in VERIS, one can only implement MBS as the difference between MTBSI and MTIR (i.e. *implementation(MBS)* = *MTBSI* − *MTIR*). This is reasonable since the definition of a blind spot between two incidents i and $i+1$ is such that $Date\_of\_Occurrence(incident_{i+1})$ − $Date\_of\_Recovery(incident_i)$. However, we can arrive at this by performing $(Date\_of\_Occurrence(incident_{i+1}) - Date\_of\_Occurrence(incident_i))$ − $(Date\_of\_Recovery(incident_i) - Date\_of\_Occurrence(incident_i))$, which is the difference between MTBSI and MTIR, assuming a uniform value for all incidents. Therefore, our implementation function f relies on this difference, and can be defined in the following manner:

$$f(MTBSI) = (100\% - \sum_{i=1}^{n}(percentage(c_i)))\ where\ c_i \geq time\_unit(MTBSI)$$

where c represents the time unit (i.e. seconds, minutes, hours, days etc.) for the Discovery-to-Containment stage in the timeline of events, and hence *percentage(c)* is the percentage of all incidents where the time to containment metric has been reported to be in that specific time unit. On the other hand, n represents the number of time units that are larger or equal to the MTBSI's time unit, as returned by the auxiliary function *time_unit*. For example, if MTBSI = 15 hours/incident interval, then $time\_unit(MTBSI) = hours$ and $n = 6$, where the six time units in this case would be $\{hours, days, weeks, months, years, never\}$. We enumerate these as $c_1, \ldots, c_6$. Note here that we also include the hours time unit, in order to err on the safe side. We also exclude those incidents with a "NA" or "unknown" values. Finally, i ranges over n.

Table 5. Percentages of incidents for each time unit of the time to containment metric (VERIS, 2013 Quarter 4)

Time unit	Seconds	Minutes	Hours	Days	Weeks	Months	Years	Never
Percentage (%)	2.17	5.07	42.03	29.00	7.97	7.97	2.17	3.62

Considering the 2013Q4 version of the dataset, we have the following percentages of incidents for each time unit of the time to containment metric, as shown in Table 5.

These numbers are based on a dataset size of 2476 incidents. Going back to the example above of MTBSI = 15 hours/incident interval, one can calculate f as follows:

$$f(15 \ hours/incident \ interval) = (100 - \sum_{i=1}^{6}(percentage(c_i)))\%$$
$$where \ c_i \geq time\_unit(15 \ hours/incident \ interval)$$
$$= (100 - (percentage(hours) + percentage(days) +$$
$$percentage(weeks) + percentage(months) +$$
$$percentage(years) + percentage(never)))\%$$
$$= (100 - (42.03 + 29 + 7.97 + 7.97 + 2.17 + 3.62))\%$$
$$= 7.24\%$$

This means that the organisation, according to its reported MTBSI value of 15 hours/incident interval, will only be fully ready in 7.24% cases of security incidents based on the data provided in the VERIS dataset. In 92.76% of cases, the organisation may/would struggle to cope with new security incidents according to the blind spot readiness metric. On the other hand, if for example the MTBSI was 15 weeks instead, then the above value returned by f would rise to 78.27%.

5.2   Implementing the AMBS Metric

The second implementation we introduce will simply be an implementation of the AMBS metric. Recall that the AMBS metric is simply dividing the length of the MTIR metric by the length of the MTBSI metric, as depicted in Fig. 5.

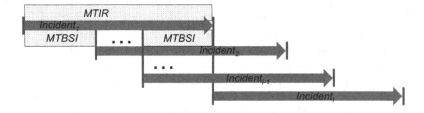

Fig. 5. A depiction of the ratio of MTIR to MTBSI

In addition to showing the ratio of the two metrics, it turns out that this definition can be used to estimate the minimum and maximum number of incidents that an organisation will have to deal with at any one time. One can deduce this fact from considering that the start of every MTBSI period signals the start of a new security incident. Therefore, if one was to fix a time frame within which one could count the number of MTBSI periods, then this would also imply the number of incidents within that time frame.

The latter case of the maximum number of incidents is particularly of interest from an incident readiness point of view, as it provides the management team some idea of the scale of resources required to tackle such events. The minimum number, on the other hand, will provide an indication of what level of resource relaxation the organisation can reach.

We start first by defining the following auxiliary function, f_{aux2}:

$$f_{aux2}(MTBSI, c) = \{\lceil min(c)/MTBSI \rceil, \lceil max(c)/MTBSI \rceil\}$$

which returns a multiset (bag) of two elements. These elements are the minimum and maximum number of incidents the organisation will be recovering from at any one time, corresponding to its specific value of MTBSI and the time unit, c, of the *time-to-containment* metric (i.e. the MTIR metric) as defined in VERIS. The MTBSI value is necessary here, so this has to be supplied by the organisation. However, the time unit c is ranged over all the meaningful time units defined in VERIS (i.e. days, hours, weeks etc.).

We calculate these numbers as the ceiling ("the gallows") ratio between the minimum and maximum values we approximate for c as explained below and the supplied value for MTBSI. This is needed since we consider that a fraction of an incident is safer approximated to a whole incident (i.e. next integer up).

We next explain how $min(c)$ and $max(c)$ are defined. Since c itself is only a time unit due to the lack of concrete date/time information on VERIS-recorded incidents, we require a 2-point time value concretisation of this abstract time unit. We do this based on the following ranges (assuming a month is 4.35 weeks):

$range$(seconds) $= [1\,s, 60\,s)$
$range$(minutes) $= [1\,min, 60\,min)$
$range$(hours) $= [1\,h, 24\,h]$
$range$(days) $= [1\,day, 7\,days)$
$range$(weeks) $= [1\,week, 4.35\,weeks)$
$range$(months) $= [1\,month, 12\,months)$
$range$(years) $= [1\,year, \infty\,years)$
$range$(never) $= [\infty\,years, \infty\,years]$

Note that we do not consider the case of "never", since this will result in dividing ∞ by MTBSI, which returns an infinite number of incidents. Since c effectively provides a *time window* within which the maximum and minimum number of incidents are approximated, providing an infinite time window will naturally lead to an infinite number of minimum and maximum incidents. We do not consider this information meaningful for understanding an organisation's readiness in tackling those periods of time when number of incidents is at its maximum.

Let's consider now an example of how f_{aux2} works. We assume that we are calculating the function for the case of $c = $ Weeks, then we need to consider the following two points in time: At week 1 and at week 4.35. This is because any less than 1 week the metric would turn to a daily time unit and any more than 4.35 weeks the metric would turn into months. If the organisation provides a value for MTBSI $= 18$ days $= 2.57$, then this means that

$$f_{aux2}(18\ Days, Weeks) = \{\lceil 1/2.57\rceil, \lceil 4.35/2.57\rceil\} = \{1, 2\}$$

On the other hand, if MTBSI was to drop to 1 day (i.e. 0.143 week), then the number of incidents would increase:

$$f_{aux2}(1\ Day, Weeks) = \{\lceil 1/0.143\rceil, \lceil 4.35/0.143\rceil\} = \{7, 31\}$$

Our function then for generating an AMBS estimation from the VERIS dataset would pair each of these two values with the percentage of incidents the c time unit occurs in VCDB:

$$f_2(MTBSI, c) = (f_{aux2}(MTBSI, c), percentage(c)) \tag{7}$$

Therefore, for the case of $c = $ Weeks, we have that $percentage(Weeks) = 7.97\%$ from [13], and hence $f_2(18\ Days, Weeks) = (\{1, 2\}, 7.97\%)$ whilst for the case of $f_2(1\ Day, Weeks) = (\{7, 31\}, 7.97\%)$. The meaning of these pairs is to provide an approximate percentage (in this case 7.97%) of the likelihood of the maximum/minimum incident number estimations being true, with reference to the data provided in VCDB and the selected c time unit. If the selected c time unit was changed, say to Days, the pair would become (for the case of MTBSI $=$ 18 days) $(\{1, 1\}, 29\%)$.

6   Conclusion and Future Work

We presented in this paper a new risk metric, called the blind spot, for expressing Cyber incident recovery readiness in organisations and IT departments. The new metric represents the gap in time between the recovery (or containment) of existing incidents and the occurrence of new incidents. We postulate that the longer the gap, the more vulnerable the organisation or IT department will be to lack of resources in tackling new incidents, hence the relationship with the concept of incident response readiness. Furthermore, we defined three variants of this new metric: the Mean Blind Spot, the Approximated Mean Blind Spot and the Ratio of Blind Spots metrics. We demonstrated how these metrics can be implemented over an open source large dataset containing information on Cyber security incidents, namely the VERIS dataset.

The significance of the VERIS dataset lies in the fact that it is community-driven, where data are collected from a variety of organisations in a wide range of industries covering small, medium and large size organisations. This ensures that the implementation of the new metrics is applicable to the wider community. However, we plan in the future to further validate the new metrics based on empirical data obtained from specific case studies for IT teams and organisations. Such specific case studies produce more accurate results, despite their scope of applicability. The application of real empirical data to this metric may expose more (specific) benefits and drawbacks for the new metrics, possibly suggesting ways to refine our initial conceptual model. Such studies will also help incorporate new factors or new metadata into the current model, particularly since the characteristics of Cyber security incidents vary over time also depending on the context. Therefore, the refinement of the metric can yield more benefits for organisations.

References

1. Black, P.E., Scarfone, K., Souppaya, M.: Cyber security metrics and measures. In: Voeller, J.G. (ed.) Wiley Handbook of Science and Technology for Homeland Security, Chap. 5, pp. 1–15. Wiley, London (2008)
2. Chew, E., Swanson, M., Stine, K., Bartol, N., Brown, A., Robinson, W.: Performance measurement guide for information security. Technical report 800–55 Revision 1, National Institute of Standards and Technology, July 2008
3. Hoo, K.J.S.: How Much is Enough? A Risk-Management Approach to Computer Security (2000)
4. The Center for Internet Security: CIS Security Metrics v1.1.0, November 2010
5. Kayworth, T., Whitten, D.: Effective information security requires a balance of social and technology factors. MIS Q. Executive **9**(3) (2012). http://ssrn.com/abstract=2058035
6. Kwon, J., Ulmer, J.R., Wang, T.: The association between top management involvement and compensation and information security breaches. J. Inf. Syst. **27**(1), 219–236 (2013). http://dx.doi.org/10.2308/isys-50339
7. P-Lippmann, R., Riordan, J.F., Yu, T.H., Watson, K.K.: Continuous security metrics for prevalent network threats: introduction and first four metrics. Technical report ESC-TR-2010-099, Massachusetts Institute of Technology (2012)
8. Payne, S.C.: A guide to security metrics. Technical report SANS Security Essentials GSEC Practical Assignment, Version 1.2e, Escal Institute of Advanced Technologies, Inc. (The SANS Institute), June 2006
9. von Solms, B., von Solms, R.: From information security to. business security? Comput. Secur. **24**(4), 271–273 (2005)
10. Swanson, M., Bartol, N., Sabato, J., Hash, J., Graffo, L.: Security metrics guide for information technology systems. Technical report 800–55, National Institute of Standards and Technology, July 2003
11. International Telecommunication Union: A Cybersecurity indicator of risk to enhance confidence and security in the use of telecommunication/information and communication technologies. Technical report X.1208, International Telecommunication Union (2014)
12. Verendel, V.: Quantified security is a weak hypothesis: a critical survey of results and assumptions. In: Proceedings of the 2009 Workshop on New Security Paradigms Workshop, NSPW 2009, pp. 37–50. ACM, New York (2009)
13. VERIZON: The Vocabulary for Event Recording and Incident Sharing (VERIS). http://veriscommunity.net/, Accessed 21 Nov 2016
14. VERIZON: VERIS Community Database. http://vcdb.org/, Accessed 21 Nov 2016

Security Risk Analysis

Quantitative Information Security Risk Estimation Using Probabilistic Attack Graphs

Pontus Johnson[1], Alexandre Vernotte[1(✉)], Dan Gorton[2], Mathias Ekstedt[1], and Robert Lagerström[1]

[1] KTH Royal Institute of Technology, Stockholm, Sweden
{pontusj,vernotte,mekstedt,robertl}@kth.se
[2] Foreseeti AB, Stockholm, Sweden
dan.gorton@foreseeti.com

Abstract. This paper proposes an approach, called pwnPr3d, for quantitatively estimating information security risk in ICT systems. Unlike many other risk analysis approaches that rely heavily on manual work and security expertise, this approach comes with built-in security risk analysis capabilities. pwnPr3d combines a network architecture modeling language and a probabilistic inference engine to automatically generate an attack graph, making it possible to identify threats along with the likelihood of these threats exploiting a vulnerability. After defining the value of information assets to their organization with regards to confidentiality, integrity and availability breaches, pwnPr3d allows users to automatically quantify information security risk over time, depending on the possible progression of the attacker. As a result, pwnPr3d provides stakeholders in organizations with a holistic approach that both allows high-level overview and technical details.

Keywords: Quantitative risk analysis · Attack graphs · Threat modeling · Network security · Information security

1 Introduction

ICT systems have become an integral part of business and life. At the same time, these systems have become extremely complex, often hosting thousands of software applications, databases, operating systems, servers, processes, data, and more. In these complex systems-of-systems exist numerous vulnerabilities waiting to be exploited by potential threat actors [27,30]. Examples include power grids being shut down[1], smart cars taken[2], and financial institutions being hit by server side [20] and denial of service attacks. This trend has been overseen by responsible authorities who step up the minimum requirements for risk management [5], including requirements of recurring risk analysis [7,8]. However, government action is slowed down by multiple contrasting figures concerning

---

[1] http://www.cnn.com/2016/02/03/politics/cyberattack-ukraine-power-grid/.
[2] http://money.cnn.com/2012/09/27/technology/bank-cyberattacks/.

© Springer International Publishing AG 2017
J. Großmann et al. (Eds.): RISK 2016, LNCS 10224, pp. 37–52, 2017.
DOI: 10.1007/978-3-319-57858-3_4

the impact of cyber attacks, which in turn makes it hard to identify new cost-effective security policies [2]. Thus, the ability to measure security is becoming a top priority in most organizations today. One example of this trend is the World Economic Forum (WEF) paper "Partnering for Cyber Resilience Towards the Quantification of Cyber Threats" published in January 2015 [9]. WEF acknowledge that cyber risk is increasingly viewed as key element of enterprise risk management and is requesting industry-specific risk models to, for example, enable cyber risk transferring.

In the individual organizations, there are many stakeholders which are interested in the management of the IT landscape and its security [11]. For some of the stakeholders, a system overview is just about enough, while others require details. So far this is also mirrored in the commonly employed tools, e.g. Visio and PowerPoint for C-level management and vulnerability scanners for network administrators. These solutions tend to focus either on providing a holistic view of the system without any connection to the actual details, or on a small part of the system, thus neglecting the bigger picture. Hence, there is a need for holistic approaches that also consider technological details [29]. However, most approaches available are driven by manual labor and require a high level of expertise, which in information security is both expensive and hard to come by [26].

pwnPr3d [18] (for *Pwn*[3] *Prediction*, pronounced [p'əʊnprɪd]) is an attacker-centric threat modeling technique for automated threats identification and quantification based on network modeling. As opposed to most other similar approaches, pwnPr3d integrates reusable analysis capability. Instead of relying on human expertise to analyze a model and decide whether it is secure or not, pwnPr3d can automatically perform this analysis. That is, the security expertise is built into the model. In its analysis, pwnPr3d generates probability distributions over the Time To Compromise (TTC) for each asset in the system, and estimates information security risk as a probability distribution of the system-wide cost of security failure. As a result, pwnPr3d provides the various stakeholders of an organization with a cyber security evaluation of their systems that is tailored to their concerns.

This paper introduces an extension to pwnPr3d's meta-modeling architecture that allows for automated quantitative information security risk estimation. A new modeling entity, called *Information*, makes it possible for users to define the atomic cost of security breaches (namely, confidentiality, integrity and availability breaches) regarding a particular piece of information. Then, a dedicated algorithm, directly integrated into the TTC calculation, computes the global quantitative information security risk depending on the possibilities presented to the attacker. The end result is a cumulative frequency distribution of the increasing cost impact of security breaches over time. The remainder of this paper is structured as follows: Sect. 2 presents related work focusing on other modeling approaches more or less similar to pwnPr3d. Then, Sect. 3 introduces

---

[3] *Pwn* is originally a misspelling of the word *own*, in information security signifying the compromise of a computer system.

the two top layers of pwnPr3d's modeling architecture. Next, Sect. 4 describes the quantitative estimation calculation of information security risk. Section 5 exemplifies the use of pwnPr3d through a motivating example. Finally, Sect. 6 concludes the paper.

2   Related Work

Several methodologies center on identifying and quantifying the security risks present on a system or system-of-systems [1,6,21,23]. These methodologies typically break down risk analysis and assessment into several activities, and provide guidance on how to efficiently perform each activity. For instance, The Australian/New Zealand Standard AS/NZS 4360 [6] sets out a risk management process that consists of six stages: Establish the context, identify the risks, analyse the risks, evaluate the risks, and finally treat the risks. The NIST SP 800-30 Risk Assessment Framework [23] proposes a more detailed process composed of nine stages, typically isolating the identification of threats and vulnerabilities. OCTAVE [1] consists of a three-phase risk assessment strategy that the evaluation team must follow to extract appropriate mitigation strategies. Sometimes, a textual or graphical language is involved to provide further guidance. CORAS [21], which follows the process defined in [6], models threat scenarios as directed acyclic graphs whose nodes and edges are weighted, i.e. assigned with likelihood values (e.g., probabilities, frequencies, or intervals of these).

A common drawback of these methodologies is that they tend to consider threats as independent events and thus do not include their potential conditional dependencies in the risk estimation. Moreover, they do not provide automated analysis, and this activity remains to be done manually.

Many approaches propose to assess the cyber security of systems and networks by modeling probabilistic attack graphs. A popular approach is to exploit the output from network vulnerability scanners to model attack graphs. MulVal [14] derives logical attack-graphs by associating the vulnerabilities extracted from scans with a probability derived from their CVSS score, which express how likely an attacker is to exploit them successfully. NAVIGATOR [4] consider identified vulnerabilities as directly exploitable by the attacker (given that he has access to the vulnerable system). The TVA tool [24] models networks in terms of security conditions and uses a database of exploits as transitions between these security conditions. Another widespread solution for the representation of attack graphs and the computation of attack probabilities is Bayesian Networks [10,28,31]. In [10], the authors translate "raw" attack graphs obtained with the TVA-tool into dynamic Bayesian networks, and convert CVSS scores of vulnerabilities to probabilities. Similarly, the authors in [31] rely on CVSS to model uncertainties in the attack structure, the actions of the attacker and the triggering of alerts. In [28], the authors use Bayesian attack graphs to estimate the security risk on network systems and produce a security mitigation plan using a genetic algorithm. Similar to pwnPr3d in ambition is P2CySeMoL [13], which is a probabilistic relational model (PRM) with the purpose to estimate the cyber security of enterprise-level system architectures.

These approaches are efficient at evaluating the cyber security of systems in terms of threat and vulnerability identification, likelihood and severity. However, they mainly focus on the technical aspects of threats and vulnerabilities, while remaining business-value-neutral. Furthermore, most of them are either manual or they indirectly rely on vulnerability scanners that, as stated above, have disputable vulnerability detection rates.

Noel et al. [25] propose to measure security risk of networks using attack graphs. The analysis takes into account associated network operational costs and attack impact costs, making it possible to combine the likelihood of an attack, its projected cost and the mitigation cost. However, the attack graph modeling and the calculation remain manual.

3   pwnPr3d's Meta-modeling Architecture

pwnPr3d is an attacker-centric threat modeling approach that allows for automated threat identification and quantification based on a model of the network under analysis, by combining a network architecture modeling language and a probabilistic inference engine. The language couples the assets of a network with attack steps that define how these assets can be compromised and what the possible consequences on the other assets are. Thus, based on a network model instance, pwnPr3d automatically generates an attack graph based on the nature of its assets and their relations. The attack graph is analyzed by considering the entry point of the attacker in the network, i.e. one or several attack steps defined as successful attempts. In addition, pwnPr3d also allows probability distributions over the Time To Compromise (TTC) for attack steps by quantifying the attack step (conditional) dependencies. Such quantitative data can be collected from various sources including surveys and studies such as [12,19]. pwnPr3d enables to automatically identify and quantify a broad set of threats, covering most of the STRIDE classification [16].

Based on a network model instance, pwnPr3d automatically generates an attack graph and analyzes it by considering the entry point of the attacker in the network, i.e. one or several attack steps defined as successful attempts. The likelihood L of assets being compromised is obtained by quantifying the attack step (conditional) dependencies and deducing probability distributions over the Time To Compromise (TTC) for attack steps. Such quantitative data can be collected from various sources including surveys and studies such as [12,19]. The cost impact I of a security incident on an information asset is defined by the users. For each asset, three types of security incident are considered: confidentiality, integrity and availability breaches. As a result, pwnPr3d quantitatively estimates information security risk R over time, depending on the calculated progression of the attacker.

pwnPr3d's modeling language is designed as a closed meta-modeling architecture, similarly to MOF [22], which offers multiple benefits when it comes to system and network modeling. One the one hand, it provides separation of concerns making it possible to capture the attack graph theory in the lower layers of the meta-model, and spreads to the higher layers. The end goal is that end users only model the assets and their relations, while all attack graph logic is encapsulated in lower layers. On the other hand, it allows a high flexibility in terms of introducing new types of assets and vulnerabilities. Components can be modeled with great level of detail for reuse as encapsulated wholes. For example, an operating system can be modeled as a composition of sub-components (applications, user accounts, network interfaces), themselves represented as a composition of sub-components. Modeling with much details enables a broad coverage of attacks, both between components and within the internals of a component. This ultimately leads to the creation of standard component libraries containing specific products (e.g., a Netgear wgr614 router).

The next sections present the terminology and modeling concepts of pwnPr3d. Only the first two layers are described, in order to keep the presentation concise.

3.1   Layer-0: Assets and Attack Graph Theory

The main purpose of *Layer-0* is to couple the components of an IT infrastructure and the attack surface of the attacker. It defines the attack graph theory, i.e. the possible progression of the attacker through attack steps, as well as TTC calculation. The metamodel of Layer-0 is depicted in Fig. 1. Its main three entities are described below.

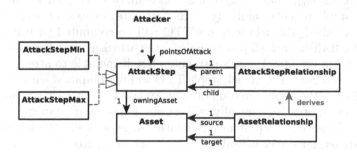

Fig. 1. Layer-0 metamodel

Asset is the class that ties together the logic of pwnPr3d. It is the class that later instantiate the core constituents of the system and the network, such as software, hardware and information. Such constituents can be related to one another through the *AssetRelationship* entity (e.g., to represent a physical connection between two computers). This is following standard object oriented modeling approaches.

Attacker represents a malicious actor that threatens the security of the system by compromising assets. In pwnPr3d, the *Attacker* entity defines the starting point of the attack. It can be connected to any *AttackStep* entity; such connections denote the source of the attack vectors. These particular attack steps thus always have a TTC that evaluates to 0.

Attack steps are actions conducted by an attacker to compromise an asset. As such, each attack step in pwnPr3d is associated to the asset it targets. Attack steps are related to one another through the *AttackStepRelationship* entity forming an attack graph. The *derives* link binds one or several *AttackStepRelationship* entities to an *AssetRelationship* entity. This is a key feature of pwnPr3d as it defines the attack graph construction theory in Layer-0, which spreads to the higher layers of the language. It thus allows for the automatic derivation of the attack graph from the behavioral relationships between assets. It is further explained in Sect. 3.2.

pwnPr3d models attack graphs as edge-weighted directed graphs where nodes represent attack steps, a subset of these nodes denotes the starting points(s) of attack, directed edges defines the possible progression of the attacker in the modeled system through the successful attempt of attack steps, and an edge weight function defines the probability distribution over time that an attacker will successfully attempt an attack step (i.e. TTC). Two kinds of attack steps are introduced in pwnPr3d: *attack step minimum* as_{min} and *attack step maximum* as_{max}, in order to specify the possible prerequisites of an attack step e.g., that the attacker needs access as well as the proper privileges in order to compromise a system. These two specializations echo the *AND* and *OR* gates that are generally used in previous works, although they have been adapted in pwnPr3d to enable the probabilistic inference of attack steps' TTC. Thereby, the attacker can attempt an as_{min} only if s/he has successfully attempted *at least one* of the attack step's parents, similarly to an OR gate. In case of several parents being compromised, the attack step's TTC will be computed with its parent's lowest TTC. If the attack step is an as_{max}, the attacker must have successfully attempted *all* of the attack step's parents before being able to attempt it, similarly to an AND gate. The attack step's TTC will be computed with its parent's highest TTC, as the approximation of true AND TTC. This approximation is a worst case, as an attacker typically will require longer time than so.

It should be noted that prerequisite relationships between attack steps should not be mistaken for direct causality. There is no guarantee that an attack will succeed as it is dependant upon a multitude of factors. The imperfect nature of exploits is one. The skill set of the attacker is another. Therefore, the edges outgoing an attack step define the possibilities that are presented to an attacker upon successful compromise of the attack step.

Calculation of TTC follows a two-steps process:

1. Each edge of the attack graph is "concretized" by getting a sample from its TTC probability distribution. The sampled value becomes the weight of the edge and represents the TTC of the edge's target attack step, given that the attacker has successfully attempted the edge's source attack step;
2. An adapted version of Dijkstra's shortest path algorithm calculates the smallest TTC value for each attack-step, depending on its ancestry. More concretely, we use Dial's Approximate Buckets implementation [3].

This process is performed N times (e.g., 500 times), and each attack step keeps track of the TTC values it has been assigned with. The end result is a frequency distribution of the successful attempt of an attack step over time.

3.2   Layer-1: Network and System-Specific Logic

Layer-1 introduces the network and system-specific logic for the attack graph generation, the various threat types that can be identified in a network, and loss calculation from CIA breaches. It uses Layer-0 as a meta-model and all the classes introduced in this layer are instances of the *Asset* entity, and each *Asset* instance contains its own set of attack steps.

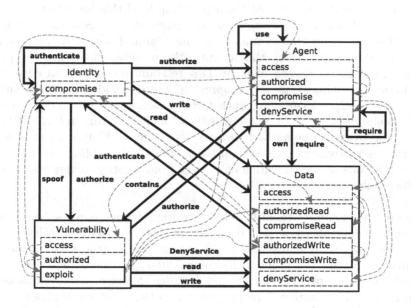

Fig. 2. The Layer-1 model including classes, class relationships, attacks steps and their dependencies. The containing entities are *Asset* instances, and the contained entities are attack steps related to their owning asset. Attack steps with dashed lines symbolize as_{min} and solid lines as_{max}. Solid edges represent behavioral associations (*AssetRelationship* instances), and dashed edges define the possible progression of the attacker from one attack step to another (*AttackStepRelationship* instances). (*Derive* associations are not represented in the figure.)

While Layer-0 encapsulates the attack graph theory, Layer-1 encapsulates the attack graph logic, i.e. how to derive the attack graph from an object model. Each Layer-1 entity owns a set of attack-steps that relate to one another, and each relationship between two entities derives a particular set of *AttackStepRelationships*. Hence, users must only instantiate the four entities (Agent, Identity, Data, Vulnerability) and their relationships, when creating a Layer-1 object model.

The model of Layer-1, depicted in Fig. 2, consists of four *Assets* instances, discussed below. For each entity, we describe its nature, its relationships with the other entities, and the attack step edges that its relationships derive.

Identities are authorization concepts that specify the restriction rules enforced in the system. Their core purpose in pwnPr3d is to specify the required privileges to read and write *Data*, control an *Agent*, exploit a *Vulnerability*. For example, only administrators are allows to read a particular file, say */etc/passwd/*.

The identity entity has one attack step: $compromised_{min}$. If the attacker compromises an identity (e.g., via credentials disclosure), s/he "assumes" this identity and gains all privileges that this identity represents on the network.

Identities have four different relationship types. First, an identity can be *authorized* to access an agent. At the attack step level this leads to the derivation of an edge from identity.*compromise* to agent.*authorize*. Second, an identity can *authenticate* as another identity (e.g., the admin of a system also has user privileges). By compromising this identity, the attacker also gains the privileges from the authenticated identity. This relationship derives an edge from administrator.*compromise* to user.*compromise*. Third, An identity can be authorized to *read* and/or *write* data. Such a relationship derives an edge between identity.*compromise* to datum.*authorizedRead* and/or datum.*authorizedWrite*. Lastly, an identity can be *authorized* to exploit a vulnerability e.g., an attacker must gain user privileges on a system to exploit a vulnerability. An *authorize* relationship leads to the derivation of an edge from identity.*compromise* to vulnerability.*authorized*.

Agents represent any active entity in the network: software, hardware, or people. An agent has four attack steps: (i) $access_{min}$ (the attacker has logical access to the agent so that it is reachable), (ii) $authorized_{min}$ (the attacker has the capability to control the agent), (iii) $compromise_{max}$: the attacker has fully assumed and taken over the agent, and (iv) $denyService_{min}$: the attacker is preventing the agent from working properly, aka a Denial-of-Service (DoS). Both *access* and *authorized* are parents of *compromise*, which specifies that in order to compromise an agent, the attacker must have logical access to it *and* the necessary privileges.

An agent may *require* another to function properly e.g., an OS requires a network interface to send data over the network. If the attacker was to perform a DoS attack on the network interface, the operating system would no longer be able to communicate. Therefore, an attack step edge is derived, from *denyService* of the required agent to *denyService* of the requiring agent. Agents may also *use* one another e.g., the network interfaces of a switch and a host use one another to exchange data. Two attack step edges are derived: one from agentA.*compromise* to agentB.*access*, and one from agentB.*compromise* to agentA.*access*.

Moreover, an agent may *require* data to function properly, e.g., in order to calculate the fastest route between two places, data about both places must be available. Hence an edge is derived from *denyService* of the datum to *denyService* of the agent. Agents may also *own* data, e.g., a database server contains sensitive data. When the attacker compromises an agent that owns data, s/he gains logical access to the data. If s/he DoS the agent, the data can no longer be accessed. Two attack step edges are derived: (1) from agent.*compromise* to datum.*access*, and (2) from agent.*denyService* to datum.*denyService*.

Lastly, an agent may *contain* a vulnerability, denoting when an asset holds a bug. If the attacker compromises the agent, s/he gets access to the vulnerability. Therefore, this attack sequence is represented by an edge from agent.*compromise* to vulnerability.*access*.

Data represents any form of information: files, transportation messages, commands, credentials, encryption, etc.

The *Data* entity has six attack steps: (i) $access_{min}$ (the attacker has logical access to the datum but still cannot read/write), (ii) $authorizedRead_{min}$ (the attacker has authorization to read the datum), (iii) $authorizedWrite_{min}$ (the attacker has authorization to write the datum), (iv) $compromiseRead_{max}$ (the attacker can read the datum), (v) $compromiseWrite_{max}$ (the attacker can write the datum), and (vi) $denyService_{min}$ (the attacker denies access to the datum). *access* and *authorizedRead* are parents of *compromiseRead*, and *access* and *authorizedWrite* are parents of *compromiseWrite*: the attacker can read (respectively write) a datum if s/he has logical access to it and has gained read (respectively write) privileges. Such privileges can typically be obtained from the compromising of an identity (e.g. identity spoofing), or by exploiting a vulnerability that directly bypasses the access restriction.

A special kind of datum in pwnPr3d is credentials and encryption keys. These are represented through the *authenticate* relation to *Identity*. If an attacker succeeds with *compromiseRead* on a datum, s/he also compromises all the identities that the datum authenticates. Note that due to a lack of space, only a simplified representation of data is presented. An aspect that is omitted is the capability of encapsulating data to represent network messages and encrypted files.

Vulnerabilities represent flaws in the implementation or design of a system: they constitute loopholes in the rule set represented by the other assets, associations and relations. In pwnPr3d, the possible prerequisites and consequences of a vulnerability exploit are modeled rather than how the vulnerability is exploited. The fact that not all vulnerability exploits result in successful compromises is captured with the probabilities in the attack step relations. Moreover, the existence of a vulnerability may be uncertain. It may be the case for instance that the administrator has secured his system even though the manufacturer has not published a patch yet. The uncertainty of a vulnerability existence is represented as a probability distribution, which further influence the calculation of TTC.

The *Vulnerability* entity has three attack steps: (i) $accessed_{min}$ (the attacker has logical access to the vulnerability), (ii) $authorized_{min}$ (the attacker has gained the necessary privileges to exploit the vulnerability), and (iii) $exploit_{max}$ (the attacker can exploit the vulnerability).

Both *access* and *authorized* are parents of *exploit*: the attacker needs access to the vulnerability and the necessary privileges in order to exploit the vulnerability. For instance, an attacker might only be able to install a firmware rootkit if s/he is (remotely) connected to the targeted system and has user privileges.

Vulnerabilities can be exploited to *spoof* an identity for escalation of privileges, i.e. compromise it through another identity. A spoof relationship leads to the derivation of an edge from $exploit_{max}$ to the attack step $compromised_{min}$ from the spoofed identity. A vulnerability exploit can also allow an attacker to *read* (respectively *write*, i.e. data tampering) a datum (i.e. information disclosure), given logical access. Two edges are derived from this relationship: from vulnerability.*exploit* to datum.*read* and to datum.*write*. Finally, a vulnerability exploit can *authorize* access to an agent, aka bypass the restriction in place. Hence, an edge is derived from vulnerability.*exploit* to agent.*authorized*. Lastly, a vulnerability when exploited can allow an attacker to DoS the agents that contain it. An edge is derived from vulnerability.*exploit* to agent.*denyService*.

4   Extension for Quantitative Information Security Risk Estimation

Information security risk is defined in ISO/IEC 27005 as "the potential that a given threat will exploit vulnerabilities of an asset or group of assets and thereby cause harm to the organization.", that is measured "in terms of a combination of the likelihood of an event and its consequence" [17]. Formally speaking, the risk R is obtained from the product of the likelihood L of a security incident occurring times the impact I it will have on the organization ($R = L * I$).

In the previous section, we described how pwnPr3d automatically computes the likelihood of attacks in term of time to compromise: The likelihood L of assets being compromised is obtained by quantifying the attack step (conditional) dependencies and deducing probability distributions over the Time To Compromise (TTC) for attack steps. In this section, we propose an extension to pwnPr3d's class model that enables users to assign the cost value I of a security incident to information assets, reflecting the cost impact of a security incident on the corresponding asset. For each asset, three types of security incident are considered: confidentiality, integrity and availability breaches. As a result, pwnPr3d quantitatively estimates information security risk R over time, depending on the calculated progression of the attacker. This extension, as depicted in Fig. 3, consists of the introduction of a new Layer-1 element that represents information assets.

Information is considered immaterial, and as such has no direct relationship with agents, identities nor vulnerabilities. It can only indirectly relate to these through a Data entity that *represents* the information. The Data entity represents the format (e.g., XML), and the Information entity represents its meaning and its value. Hence, when an identity has read privileges on a datum, it has by extension read privileges on the information itself. Furthermore, information may be represented by multiple data stored in different places (e.g., the enterprise performs regular back-ups of a database).

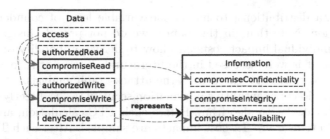

Fig. 3. Relationship between Data and Information

The Information entity can be compromised according to three attack steps, matching the CIA triad:

- $compromiseConfidentiality_{min}$: the attacker has gained logical access to one of the data that represent the information with read privileges, which gives him the possibility to access the information.
- $compromiseIntegrity_{max}$: the attacker has gained logical access to one of the data with write privileges, he can therefore compromise the integrity of the information.
- $compromiseAvailability_{max}$: the attacker has made all the data representing the information unavailable to their surroundings (e.g., through denial of service), hence compromising the information's availability. Because this is a direct technical consequence, the TTC of the attack step edge between data.*denyService* and *compromiseAvailability* is set to 0.

compromiseIntegrity and *compromiseAvailability* are as_{max}, since Information can be present in a system in multiple places. Therefore, if the attacker compromises one of the representing data, technically the information is still available/coherent. Contrariwise, $compromiseConfidentiality_{min}$ is an as_{min} because it only takes the attacker to attempt *compromiseRead* on one of the representing data to compromise the information confidentiality.

Each information instance must be valued with three attributes that express the cost impact of Confidentiality, Integrity and Availability breaches. The type of cost is reliant on the type of the attack step, i.e. *compromiseConfidentiality* relates to Confidentiality cost, *compromiseIntegrity* to Integrity cost, and *compromiseAvailability* to Availability cost. It is the users responsibility to quantify the cost impact of CIA breaches for each information instance. Indeed, evaluating such costs is an onerous and very speculative task that involves many factors [15]. One may consider immediate losses as well as delayed losses, including time sensitivity, impact on the stock market, cost of asset recovery, and so on. Deciding which factors should be considered and to what extent is a real challenge and as a result, the quantification might be quite inaccurate, regardless of the employed evaluation methodology. To palliate this inaccuracy, impact costs are defined as probability distributions. In the next section, for instance, costs are quantified using truncated normal distributions. Another option would be to use beta distributions, to model the variable level of confidence within the distribution. Note that, in this paper, we do not provide insights on how to calculate individual impact costs and how to derive probability distributions from them (as it is well discussed in the literature). Instead, the focus is solely on how these cost are aggregated w.r.t the attack-graph analysis.

The calculation of quantitative information security risk is directly integrated into the TTC calculation algorithm. Before each TTC calculation, all the probability distributions over CIA cost impacts are sampled. After each TTC calculation, the successfully attempted attack steps that are owned by Information entities are inspected to collect tuples composed of the TTC value of the attack-step and the sampled cost impact of the owning Information entity. Tuples are then ordered based on their TTC value (from soonest to latest), and their associated cost impact are cumulated: the cumulative cost of a given tuple is the sum of its initial cost and the cumulative cost of its predecessor. Once the TTC calculation algorithm has been executed N times, the obtained N collections of tuples are merged and distributed in time bins. The end result is a cumulative frequency distribution of the increasing cost impact of CIA breaches over time, depending on the progression of the attacker in the network. Users are presented with a cumulative histogram featuring the 5, 50, and 95 percentiles.

5   Motivating Example

Applying pwnPr3d on the test enterprise network involves the design of a topology model that comprises all the components and assets of the network, how they connect to one another, what the various access restrictions (e.g. firewall rules) are, what the value of information assets is, as well as the introduction of one (or several) attacker(s). Of course, the goal of full threat analysis and security risk calculation automation is only achieved when complex classes have been defined and grouped in component libraries ultimately made available to end users (e.g., someone needs to define how Windows 10 is constructed). Once the appropriate classes are available, pwnPr3d can be used for the evaluation of different design scenarios. However, high-level components and product libraries are out of the scope of this paper, the focus being on the core layers of pwnPr3d and its extension that makes it possible to compute global information security risk. Hence, it should be noted that the motivating example presented below does not reflect how end users would model their enterprise network.

Consider a snippet of a heavily simplified software development enterprise network. It is composed of a Windows 10 client host that has two level of privileges: guest and user. To get user privileges, one must know the associated credentials. The windows 10 client host is connected to a Linux server host, which stores all the source code created within the enterprise. With user privileges on the Windows 10 client host, one has access to the home folder related to the user account, and admin privileges on the Linux server host. Finally, the Windows 10 client host has a known (fictional) vulnerability that, if exploited, gives the attacker authorzed read on the user credentials of the host. In this example, the

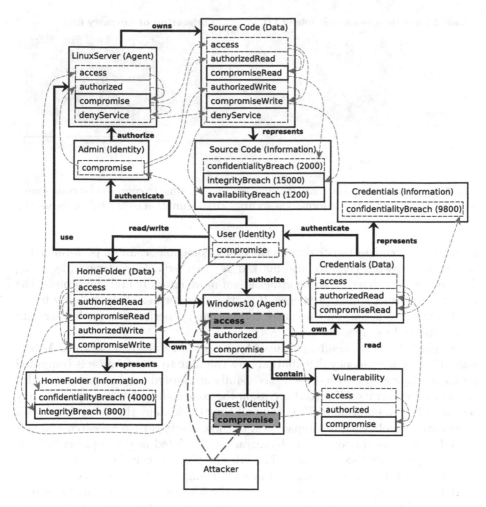

Fig. 4. pwnPr3d model of the test network, with sampled impact costs of CIA breaches

goal is to measure the possible progression of the attacker and the corresponding estimation of information security risk given that the s/he has logical access to the Windows 10 client host, with guest privileges. It is defined in the model with two *startingPoint* relations from the attacker to the concerned objects. The pwnPr3d object model for this example is depicted in Fig. 4, designed using pwnPr3d's layer 1 meta-model.

Because the attacker has logical access to the Windows host with guest privileges, the host is considered compromised. Therefore, the attacker can now exploit the vulnerability in ordeer to obtain read authorization on the user credentials. If performed, the attacker has the possibility to become *User* on the Windows host. Since credentials are data, a cost of 9800 has been set in case of a confidentiality breach, which gets marked as "reached". The attacker also gets to

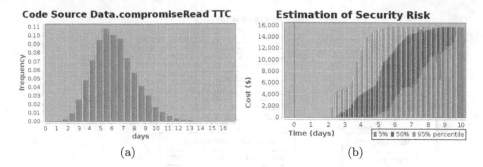

Fig. 5. pwnPr3d result: frequency distribution over the time to compromise code source data (a) and quantitative information security risk estimation of the test network (b)

possibility to read and write data in the user's home folder, and if performed, the associated breaches cost are also marked as "reached". Furthermore, by being *User* on the Windows host, the attacker can move laterally and compromise the Linux server with admin privileges. If so, the attacker has the possibility to get read/write permissions on the source code. Again, if performed, further security cost is marked as "reached".

Figure 5 shows the results produced by pwnPr3d for the test network. As presented in *(a)*, a frequency distribution over the time to compromise is computed for each attack step that has been successfully attempted by the attacker. In this example, the average TTC read access on the code source data is approximately 6 days. The combination of TTC from all the attack steps that are related with information assets with the impact cost of these assets is then collected and presented to users in the form of an histogram, as depicted in (b), representing the increasing security risk over time. The 5th and 95th percentiles are impact cost distributions for each time span (a time span being a tenth of day). For example, at day 6 in the figure, the impact cost of the 5% lowest cost calculations tops at around $2000. It means that, if there were 1000 calculations, ranked from lowest overall impact cost to higher overall impact cost after 6 days, the 5th percentile is the overall impact cost of the 50th lowest calculation. Similarly, the 95th percentile is the overall impact cost of the 50th highest calculation.

6   Conclusions

pwnPr3d is an attacker-centric probabilistic threat modeling technique for automated risk identification and quantification based on a topology model of the system under analysis. The components of the system, depending on their nature and how they relate to one another, are automatically coupled with attack steps that define how these assets can be compromised: the threat analysis is built-in and no security expertise is required from the users. An attack graph is calculated from the topology model and populated with probability distributions over the Time To Compromise (TTC) on each of its attack steps, thus defining the likelihood of the identified threats to exploit a vulnerability. Once users have defined the value of information assets to their organization, pwnPr3d automatically computes a quantitative estimation of information security risk over time, depending on the calculated progression of the attacker.

Future work is directed toward two research directions: (i) the extension of the language to include complex components and products for users to simply instantiate, and (ii) the extension of risk analysis to tangible assets in order to improve its overall accuracy and precision. Furthermore, a thorough experimentation on real-life systems is ongoing to validate the approach.

Acknowledgments. The work presented in this paper has received funding from the European Unions Seventh Framework Programme for research, technological development and demonstration under grant agreement no. 607109 as well as the Swedish Civil Contingencies Agency (MSB) through the research centre on Resilient Information and Control Systems (RICS).

References

1. Alberts, C.J., Dorofee, A.: Managing Information Security Risks: The OCTAVE Approach. Addison-Wesley Longman Publishing Co., Inc. (2002)
2. Armin, J., Thompson, B., Ariu, D., Giacinto, G., Roli, F., Kijewski, P.: 2020 cybercrime economic costs: No measure no solution. In 10th International Conference on Availability, Reliability and Security (ARES), pp. 701–710. IEEE (2015)
3. Cherkassky, B.V., Goldberg, A.V., Radzik, T.: Shortest paths algorithms: theory and experimental evaluation. Math. Program. **73**(2), 129–174 (1996)
4. Chu, M., Ingols, K., Lippmann, R., Webster, S., Boyer, S.: Visualizing attack graphs, reachability, and trust relationships with navigator. In: Proceedings of the 7th International Symposium on Visualization for Cyber Security, pp. 22–33. ACM (2010)
5. European Commission. Towards a general policy on the fight against cyber crime (2007). http://eur-lex.europa.eu/legal-content/EN/TXT/PDF/?uri=CELEX:52007DC0267. Accessed 5 March 2017
6. Cooper, D.: The australian and new zealand standard on risk management, as/nzs 4360: 2004. Tutorial Notes: Broadleaf Capital International Pty Ltd, pp. 128–151 (2004)
7. ECB. Recommendations for the security of internet payments (2015). https://www.ecb.europa.eu/pub/pdf/other/recommendationssecurityinternetpay mentsoutcomeofpcfinalversionafterpc201301en.pdf, Accessed 5 March 2017
8. FFIEC. Supplement to authentication in an internet banking environment (2011). https://www.fdic.gov/news/news/financial/2011/fil11050.pdf. Accessed 5 March 2017
9. W. E. Forum. Industry agenda. partnering for cyber resilience - towards the quantification of cyber threats, January 2015. http://www3.weforum.org/docs/WEFUSA_QuantificationofCyberThreats_Report2015.pdf. Accessed 5 March 2017
10. Frigault, M., Wang, L., Singhal, A., Jajodia, S.: Measuring network security using dynamic Bayesian network. In: Proceedings of the 4th ACM Workshop on Quality of Protection, pp. 23–30. ACM (2008)

11. Goodyear, M., Goerdel, H.T., Portillo, S., Williams, L.: Cybersecurity management in the states: The emerging role of chief information security officers. Available at SSRN **2187412** (2010)
12. Holm, H.: A large-scale study of the time required to compromise a computer system. IEEE Trans. Dependable Secure Comput. **11**(1), 2–15 (2014)
13. Holm, H., Shahzad, K., Buschle, M., Ekstedt. M.: P cysemol: predictive, probabilistic cyber security modeling language. IEEE Trans. Dependable Secure Comput. **12**(6), 626–639 (2015)
14. Homer, J., Zhang, S., Ou, X., Schmidt, D., Du, Y., Rajagopalan, S.R., Singhal, A.: Aggregating vulnerability metrics in enterprise networks using attack graphs. J. Comput. Secur. **21**(4), 561–597 (2013)
15. Hoo, K.J.S.: How much is enough? A risk management approach to computer security. Stanford University Stanford, Calif (2000)
16. Howard, M., LeBlanc, D.: Writing secure code, 2nd edn. (2002)
17. E. ISO. Iec 27005: 2011 (en) information technology-security techniques-information security risk management switzerland. ISO/IEC (2011)
18. Johnson, P., Vernotte, A., Ekstedt, M., Lagerström, R.: pwnpr3d: an attack-graph-driven probabilistic threat-modeling approach. In: 11th International Conference on Availability, Reliability and Security (ARES). IEEE (2016)
19. Jonsson, E., Olovsson, T.: A quantitative model of the security intrusion process based on attacker behavior. IEEE Trans. Softw. Eng. **23**(4), 235–245 (1997)
20. Kaspersky. The great bank robbery: Carbanak cybergang steals $1bn from 100 financial institutions worldwide (2015). http://usa.kaspersky.com/about-us/press-center/press-releases/2015/great-bank-robbery-carbanak-cybergang-steals-1-billion-100-fina. Accessed 5 March 2017
21. Lund, M.S., Solhaug, B., Stølen, K.: Model-Driven Risk Analysis: The CORAS Approach. Springer Science & Business Media, Heidelberg (2010)
22. Meta object facility (MOF) 2.5 core specification (2015). http://www.omg.org/spec/MOF/2.5/
23. S. NIST. 800–30. Risk management guide for information technology systems, pp. 800–30 (2002)
24. Noel, S., Elder, M., Jajodia, S., Kalapa, P., O'Hare, S., Prole, K.: Advances in topological vulnerability analysis. In: Conference For Homeland Security, CATCH 2009. Cybersecurity Applications Technology, pp. 124–129, March 2009
25. Noel, S., Jajodia, S., Wang, L., Singhal, A.: Measuring security risk of networks using attack graphs. Int. J. Next Gener. Comput. **1**(1), 135–147 (2010)
26. Nyanchama, M.: Enterprise vulnerability management and its role in information security management. Inform. Syst. Secur. **14**(3), 29–56 (2005)
27. Ponemon Institute. Cost of cyber crime report (2013)
28. Poolsappasit, N., Dewri, R., Ray, I.: Dynamic security risk management using Bayesian attack graphs. IEEE Trans. Dependable Secure Comput. **9**(1), 61–74 (2012)
29. Soomro, Z.A., Shah, M.H., Ahmed, J.: Information security management needs more holistic approach: a literature review. Int. J. Inf. Manage. **36**(2), 215–225 (2016)
30. Verizon. Data breach investigations report (2014)
31. Xie, P., Li, J.H., Ou, X., Liu, P., Levy, R.: Using Bayesian networks for cyber security analysis. In: 2010 IEEE/IFIP International Conference on Dependable Systems and Networks (DSN), pp. 211–220. IEEE (2010)

Fast and Optimal Countermeasure Selection
for Attack Defence Trees

Steve Muller[1,2,3(✉)], Carlo Harpes[1], and Cédric Muller[1]

[1] itrust consulting s.à r.l., Niederanven, Luxembourg
`{steve.muller,harpes,cedric.muller}@itrust.lu`
[2] University of Luxembourg, Luxembourg City, Luxembourg
[3] Telecom Bretagne, Cesson-Sévigné, France

Abstract. Risk treatment is an important part of risk management, and deals with the question which security controls shall be implemented in order to mitigate risk. Indeed, most notably when the mitigated risk is low, the costs engendered by the implementation of a security control may exceed its benefits. The question becomes particularly interesting if there are several countermeasures to choose from.

A promising candidate for modeling the effect of defensive mechanisms on a risk scenario are attack–defence trees. Such trees allow one to compute the risk of a scenario before and after the implementation of a security control, and thus to weigh its benefits against its costs.

A naive approach for finding an optimal set of security controls is to try out all possible combinations. However, such a procedure quickly reaches its limits already for a small number of defences.

This paper presents a novel branch-and-bound algorithm, which skips a large part of the combinations that cannot lead to an optimal solution. The performance is thereby increased by several orders of magnitude compared to the pure brute–force version.

Keywords: Attack-defence tree · Return On Security Investment · Optimal defences · Risk treatment optimisation · Branch and bound algorithm

1 Introduction

Several risk methodologies exist [1] that assist the risk assessor in identifying and handling risk, by providing exhaustive libraries of risk scenarios and/or defensive mechanisms. Those methodologies require organisations to conduct a risk assessment, which permits them to identify the risks that have to be mitigated. However, they do not prescribe in detail how organisations should put such a process into practise, leaving them enough freedom to choose an approach that fits their needs and requirements. There are several frameworks (such as ISO/IEC 27005 [2], IT-Grundschutz [3], MAGERIT [4] or EBIOS [5]) and commercial tools (such as TRICK Service[1]) that assist stakeholders in taking

---

[1] www.itrust.lu/products.

© Springer International Publishing AG 2017
J. Großmann et al. (Eds.): RISK 2016, LNCS 10224, pp. 53–65, 2017.
DOI: 10.1007/978-3-319-57858-3_5

decisions for putting security controls in place. As for research, Attack–Defence Trees [6] constitute a visual and very intuitive technique for analysing a risk scenario in greater detail. They are a generalisation of ordinary attack trees [7]: The latter encode, in a tree structure, how an attack (the root node) can be achieved through intermediary attacks (its child nodes), so each branch adds further refinement the parent attack – see Fig. 1 for an example. In contrast, attack–*defence* trees also include the defensive mechanisms used to mitigate these attacks. More precisely, the associated defence nodes are appended as specially marked nodes to the attack nodes they protect from. These defences again face attacks on their own, which try to disable the countermeasures. In fact, attack–defence trees adopt the game-theoretic concept of two players, opponent and proponent, who alternately try to defeat each other [8]. Figure 2 depicts a simple attack–defence tree.

Recent research work by Gadyatskaya et al. [9] shows how attack–defence trees can be combined with existent libraries (such as ISO/IEC 27002 [10]) to determine the security controls an organisation shall implement. Indeed, when a given set of controls is implemented, it will reduce the overall risk, but also comes at a certain cost. Or, in other words, every selection of countermeasures comes with a certain return after a certain investment. However, if the investment outweighs the return, it is not sensible to mitigate the risk in the first place. The related optimisation problem consists in finding those controls that have the best return on investment.

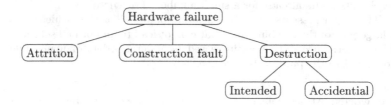

Fig. 1. A sample attack tree depicting the possible reasons of hardware failure.

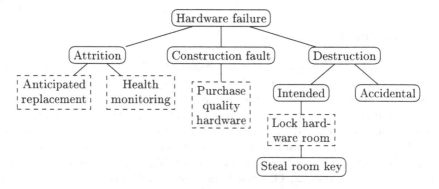

Fig. 2. A sample attack–defence tree, extending the example in Fig. 1. The dashed nodes are defence nodes.

The authors semi-automatically embed the security controls from ISO/IEC 27002 [10] as defence nodes into an existing attack tree. A simple brute-force program then iterates over all possible combinations of implementing those security controls, trying to find the strategy which maximises the return on investment. They have also developed a tool, ADTop, to demonstrate the work flow described in their paper. However, such an approach is very resource-intensive, and thus only works for very small input data. In this paper, we improve on their work and propose a faster and memory-saving algorithm for finding the set of security controls that minimises both risk and the security costs in an optimal way.

Other authors have proposed similar approaches and algorithms. Dewri et al. [11] propose a genetic algorithm that optimises a multi-objective function taking into account the attack probability and the implementation costs. However, they model defensive mechanisms as objects that mitigate an attack *completely*, which is far from reality. In contrast, Roy et al. [12] propose a model based on attack–defence trees and express the added-value of implementing a security control as return-on-investment, taking into account the risk reduction and the implementation costs. They propose a branch-and-bound algorithm, but it requires that at least one countermeasure is selected for each attack, which may not be necessarily sensible if the risk associated to that attack is already low.

This paper is organised as follows. Section 2 introduces the optimisation problem and the underlying model. Section 3 presents and deliberates the algorithm, as well as its performance. A real-world case study is used to substantiate the need for the algorithm in Sect. 4. A conclusion is drawn in Sect. 5.

2   The Optimisation Problem

2.1   Attack–Defence Trees

An attack–defence tree is defined [13] as a tree graph consisting of two kinds of nodes:

- **attack** nodes, characterised by a name and a success probability $p \in [0, 1]$;
- **defence** nodes, characterised by a name, an effectiveness $e \in [0, 1]$ and a cost $c \geq 0$.

The parameters have the following meaning:

- The **success probability** expresses the likelihood that the attacker succeeds in accomplishing the attack. If the node is a leaf, the success probability is part of the input. Otherwise, it is computed according to the rules defined below.
- The **effectiveness** expresses the degree (as a factor) to which the countermeasure reduces the attack probability. The value 0 indicates that it is entirely useless, 1 represents complete mitigation of the attack. The effectiveness is part of the input.
- The **cost** is expressed in financial terms and represents the cost engendered by the implementation of the defence. The cost is also part of the input.

The root node of an attack–defence tree is always an attack goal. Attack nodes can have subordinated attacks (that add more refinement) and defences (that defend against this attack). Defence nodes can only have subordinated attacks (that weaken the countermeasures).

For simplicity, this paper does not consider counter-attacks against defences. Thus, in the following, defences are assumed to have no subordinate child nodes.

Moreover, the set of child attacks can be 'disjunctive' or 'conjunctive', meaning that the parent attack consists of achieving *any* or *all* of the child attacks, respectively. Similarly, the set of child defences can be 'disjunctive' or 'conjunctive', meaning that *any* or *all* of the defences are required to protect from the attack, respectively.

All attacks and defences in the tree are assumed to be independent. This assumption is made to simplify the computations, and might not reflect reality. To take dependencies into consideration, more general models have to be considered, such as Bayesian networks – these are out of the scope of this paper, though.

2.2   Multi-purpose Defences

A defence can protect from several attacks, though possibly with a different effectiveness. For instance, digital e-mail signatures prevent content manipulation by third parties in a very effective fashion. At the same time, they verify the sender's identity and defend against impersonation attacks. However, the effectiveness is a bit lower in this case, since the recipient cannot be entirely sure that the sender is the real person he expected, for the latter could hack himself into that person's computer.

In this paper, defences are allowed to protect from multiple attacks, possibly with different effectiveness values. That is, if one decides to implement such a defence, and thus include it into the attack–defence tree, it will be appended to *all* applicable attacks.

2.3   Rules of Calculation

For an attack α, let $p(\alpha)$ denote its success probability. For a defence δ, let $c(\delta)$ denote its cost, and $e(\delta)$ its effectiveness.

When no defence mechanisms are present, and assuming that all attacks in the tree are independent, the following basic probability rules hold for a non-leaf attack node α.

$$
p(\alpha) = \begin{cases} \displaystyle\prod_i p(i) & \text{if } \alpha \text{ is conjunctive} \\ \displaystyle 1 - \prod_i (1 - p(i)) & \text{if } \alpha \text{ is disjunctive,} \end{cases}
$$

where i iterates over all child attack nodes of α. If a defence δ is in place, by definition of the effectiveness, it reduces the success probability by a factor

$$1 - e(\delta).$$

Similarly, if a set of defences Δ is in place, the success probability will be reduced by $1 - e(\Delta)$, where

$$e(\Delta) := \begin{cases} \displaystyle\prod_{\delta \in \Delta} e(\delta) & \text{if } \Delta \text{ is conjunctive} \\ 1 - \displaystyle\prod_{\delta \in \Delta} (1 - e(\delta)) & \text{if } \Delta \text{ is disjunctive,} \end{cases}$$

assuming that defences reduce the success probability independently from each other. So in summary, if a set Δ is implemented for an attack α, the recursive computation rule is given by

$$p(\alpha) = (1 - e(\Delta)) \cdot \begin{cases} \displaystyle\prod_{i} p(i) & \text{if } \alpha \text{ is conjunctive} \\ 1 - \displaystyle\prod_{i}(1 - p(i)) & \text{if } \alpha \text{ is disjunctive.} \end{cases} \tag{1}$$

The recursion ends at the leaf nodes, for which the probability is fixed and part of the input.

2.4 Optimisation Problem

Implementing a defence δ reduces the success probability, but also comes at a cost $c(\delta)$. It is not a-priori obvious whether it is profitable to implement a specific defence, because it could be wiser to select one or several others that come at a lower cost. The problem thus consists in finding those defences that reduce the success probability by a decent amount, but still come at a reasonably low cost.

In order to solve this multivariate optimisation problem, the Return On Security Investment (ROSI) is chosen as score function. It is defined as

$$\text{ROSI} := \underbrace{\text{impact} \cdot (\text{initial probability} - \text{final probability})}_{\text{return (risk reduction)}} - \underbrace{\text{sum of costs}}_{\text{investment}},$$

where 'initial' and 'final' are understood to be before and after the implementation of all defences. A strategy is said to be optimal if it maximises the ROSI. Note that there are many ways to define the ROSI (see e.g. [14]); this definition was chosen because of its intuitive meaning and its simplicity.

Formally, denote the set of all available defences by D. An *assignment* is a function $x : D \rightarrow \{0, 1\}$ which states whether each defence δ shall be implemented $(x(\delta) = 1)$ or not $(x(\delta) = 0)$. The ROSI can mathematically be expressed as

$$\text{ROSI}(x) := \mathcal{I} \cdot (\mathcal{P}_0 - \mathcal{P}(x)) - \sum_{\delta \in D} x(\delta) \cdot c(\delta), \tag{2}$$

where $\mathcal{I}$ is the (constant) impact of the risk scenario, $\mathcal{P}(x)$ is the success probability of the attack–defence tree after implementing all defences with $x(\cdot) = 1$, and $\mathcal{P}_0$ is the (constant) success probability of the attack–defence tree (thus without any defences). The probabilities are calculated using the formula given in Sect. 2.3. The optimisation problem then reads as

$$\text{Find} \quad x : D \to \{0, 1\} \tag{3}$$
$$\text{that maximises} \quad \text{ROSI}(x).$$

3 Branch and Bound Algorithm

The optimisation problem can be solved in several ways. One possibility would be to turn $\text{ROSI}(x)$ as defined in Eq. (2) into a linear function and apply standard linear programming algorithms [15] on it. Such an approach has been proposed and described by Roy et al. [12]. While this technique works in theory, the size of the linear program exceeds the practical limits of feasibility very quickly. For the case study presented in Sect. 4 below, the linear program would have a size of 2^{16} variables.

The proposed algorithm is given in Algorithm 1 and basically enumerates all possible combinations of applying defences. However, it skips all sets of combinations that are known not to contain any solutions. Note that it will never skip a valid combination; this is proved below. The algorithm is invoked with $D_p := \emptyset$ and an empty map $x : \emptyset \to \{0, 1\}$. The attack–defence tree T, the set of defences D and the effectiveness values e remain constant throughout the algorithms.

Note that if it was not for lines 1–3, Algorithm 1 were just a recursive brute-force algorithm that tries out all possible ways of selecting defences. The innovation (and performance optimisation) lies in the lines 1–3.

The idea is to skip a recursion step whenever it is known that it cannot yield a viable combination of selecting defences. The skip criterion in line 1 originates from the following observation. Equation (1) reveals that whenever a defence is added to the attack–defence tree, the success probability of *any* attack node will either decrease or at least remain the same. In particular, the same is true for the global success probability of the tree.

Note that whenever the algorithm enters a recursion step, all non-processed defences are set to 'unselected'; this is assured by the start condition and line 16. Thus, all later (i.e. deeper) recursion steps will end up with a lower or equal overall success probability for the attack–defence tree. By consequence, once the probability is no longer sufficiently reduced to cover the costs (i.e., once a defence is no longer profitable), it will not be profitable for all later combinations, either. Which means that all subsequent combinations are known to be invalid *a-priori*, so they can be skipped.

3.1 Performance

The performance gain depends on the structure of the attack–defence tree. A stress test was conducted on a tree consisting of 81 nodes and 90 defences, each

---

Algorithm 1. Branch and bound algorithm BNBA

Input: Attack–defence tree T with attack nodes A
Input: Set of defences D
Input: Effectiveness values $e : A \times D \to [0,1]$
Input: Set of already processed defences $D_p \subseteq D$
Input: Partial selection strategy $x : D_p \to \{0,1\}$
Output: Selection strategy x_{opt} that maximises ROSI$(\cdot)$

1: **if** there is $\delta \in D_p$ that is no longer profitable (cf. Algorithm 2) **then**
2:    **abort** current recursion step
3: **end if**

4: **if** $D_p = D$ **then**
5:    $v \leftarrow \mathbf{ROSI}(x)$
6:    **if** v is largest ROSI seen so far **then**
7:       $x_{\text{opt}} \leftarrow x$
8:    **end if**
9: **else**
10:    $\delta \leftarrow$ any defence *not* in D_p
11:    $D_p \leftarrow D_p \cup \{\delta\}$

12:    ' Try selecting the defence
13:    $x(\delta) \leftarrow 1$
14:    BNBA(T, D, e, D_p, x)

15:    ' Try not selecting the defence
16:    $x(\delta) \leftarrow 0$
17:    BNBA(T, D, e, D_p, x)

18:    ' Remove δ again; this allows the re-use of D_p among all recursive calls
19:    $D_p \leftarrow D_p \setminus \{\delta\}$
20: **end if**

---

of which is applied to every attack. The resulting attack–defence tree has thus $81 \cdot 90 = 7290$ defence nodes. Note that in a concrete case, not every defence would be applicable for every attack, and by consequence, the problem would be simpler. The effectiveness values $e : A \times D \to [0,1]$ were chosen randomly.

If one comments out lines 1–3 in Algorithm 1, one obtains a pure brute-force algorithm that tries out all 2^{90} combinations. Executing it for the first 2^{20} combinations took $107.42\,\text{s}$ in our implementation; so it would need $1.27 \cdot 10^{23}\,\text{s}$ ($4 \cdot 10^{15}$ years) to finish. On contrast, the optimised variant terminated within $895\,\text{s}$ ($15\,\text{min}$), having evaluated only $1,748,272$ combinations (which is approximately a 10^{-21} part).

Algorithm 1 can be implemented in such a way that it uses constant memory in the course of its execution. This can be achieved by using a `stack` data structure for D_p and a fixed-size array for x; both D_p and x are shared among all recursive calls of the algorithm. In our implementation the memory usage was approximately 20 MiB for the tree described above.

Algorithm 2. Determine if a defence is profitable

Input: Defence δ
Input: Cost $c(\delta)$ of defence δ
Input: Impact $\mathcal{I}$ of risk scenario
Input: Partial selection strategy $x : D_p \rightarrow \{0, 1\}$
Output: **true** if δ is profitable, **false** otherwise

1: **if** $x(\delta) = 0$ **then**
2:     **return true**
3: **else**
4:     ' Extend x to all of D
5:     $x(\delta') \leftarrow 0$ for all $\delta' \in D \setminus D_p$

6:     $x(\delta) \leftarrow 0$
7:     $v_0 \leftarrow \text{ROSI}(x)$

8:     $x(\delta) \leftarrow 1$
9:     $v_1 \leftarrow \text{ROSI}(x)$

10:     ' δ is profitable iff the residual risk is lower when δ is implemented
11:     **if** $v_1 \cdot \mathcal{I} + c(\delta) < v_0 \cdot \mathcal{I}$ **then**
12:         **return true**
13:     **else**
14:         **return false**
15:     **end if**
16: **end if**

The tests were conducted on a standard laptop with a i7-6700HQ processor (2.6 GHz). Our implementation of the algorithm ran on a single core, although it can be modified in such a way that it supports multi-threading, as well.

4 Case-Study

The methodology presented in [9], together with the new Algorithm 1, is used to determine those ISO 27002 [10] security controls that have the largest added-value for the 'ÉpStan' project.

ÉpStan, which is short for *Épreuves Standardisées* (standardised exams), is Luxembourg's national programme to monitor the quality of the educational system of secondary school. To achieve this, standardised exams are conducted in selected classes all over the country, and the results are analysed to spot topics that are not well covered by the school programme.

Since the tests are meant to rate the educational system, rather than the individual students' performance, the results should under no circumstances be linked to the individuals. There are four parties involved in the process:

- The *Government* provides the standardised exams.
- The *schools* organise and conduct the exams.
- The *University of Luxembourg* is responsible for evaluating the results.

– *itrust consulting* acts as a trusted third party and pseudonymisation service between the Government and the University of Luxembourg. Its role is to assure that neither of them can link results to an individual student. This is achieved by issuing a pseudonym for each student, which is used by the schools to exchange the exam results with the University. itrust consulting never obtains any exam result.

The process is designed in such a way that neither the University, nor the Government, nor itrust consulting can link exam results to individual students. Although every entity only knows part of the necessary information, an attacker could get (legally or not) data from multiple entities, and reconstruct the link between result and student.

A brainstorming session led to the identification of an exhaustive list of attack scenarios, all of which have been encoded in an attack tree consisting of 81 attack nodes. Figure 3 shows a small excerpt.

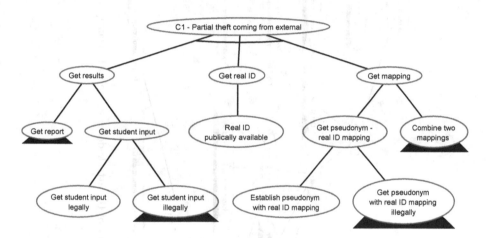

Fig. 3. An excerpt of the attack tree for the risk scenario where an attack can link exam results to a student.

The second step consisted in determining the ISO 27002 [10] controls that reduce the success probability of some of the identified attacks. In total 16 controls were retained. Moreover, the effectiveness was estimated in a brainstorming process for each of the retained defences and each of the applicable attacks. The resulting effectiveness matrix $e : A \times D \rightarrow [0,1]$ had 58 non-zero values and is depicted in Table 1.

ADTop (see [9]) required 54.2 s and over 1 GiB of memory to find the optimal attack–defence tree. A C# implementation of Algorithm 1 proposed the same set of defences within 0.36 s, having tried out 12,496 combinations (19% out of the 2^{16} possible). The memory usage was 20 MiB. An excerpt of the full attack–defence tree is depicted in Fig. 4.

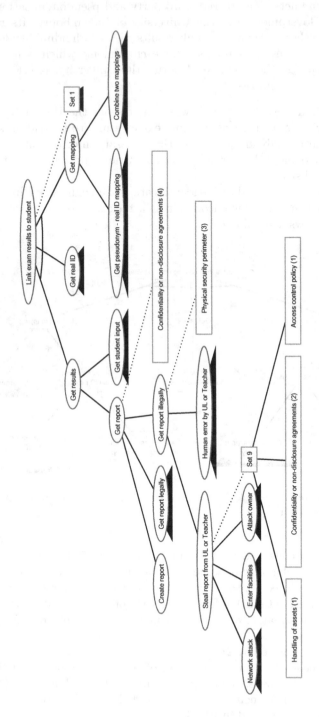

Fig. 4. An excerpt of the attack–defence tree with security controls appended.

Table 1. An excerpt of the effectiveness matrix, which has (16 defences × 81 attacks). Values indicated are in %.

	Confidentiality or non-disclosure agreements	Access control policy	Network controls	Physical security perimeter	Segregation of duties	Handling of assets	Password management system	Restrictions on software installation	Removal or adjustment of access rights	Secure disposal or re-use of equipment	Management of technical vulnerabilities	Event logging	Administrator and operator logs	Change management	Capacity management	Information security roles and responsibilities
Combine two mappings	50			5												
Human error by UL or Teacher	20	20														
Human error by TTP	20	20														
Steal student input from EpStan party	5	10			5	2										
Get pseudonym - real ID mapping		1			10	2			1							
Get student input illegally	5			5												
Network attack			50										2	2		
Steal from TTP or School or Teacher	5	10			5	2										
...																
Steal pseudonym from UL or TTP	5	10			5	2			0.5							
Human error by TTP or School or Teacher	20															
Steal report from UL or Teacher	5	10			5	2										
Get or steal temp ID from Post						2										
Link exam results to students			5	5	10	1	20	8	1		5	1	1	2	2	0.01
Get real ID	2	10	5			2										
Get report legally	5				5	2										
Steal item	2			20												

Out of the original 16 defences, the following 9 have been proposed for implementation by the algorithm.

- Handling of assets (Sect. 8.2.3)
- Password management system (Sect. 9.4.3)
- Physical security perimeter (Sect. 11.1.1)
- Capacity management (Sect. 12.1.3)
- Management of technical vulnerabilities (Sect. 12.6.1)
- Restrictions on software installation (Sect. 12.6.2)
- Network controls (Sect. 13.1.1)
- Confidentiality or non-disclosure agreements (Sect. 13.2.4)
- Access control policy (Sect. 9.1.1)

This solution reduces the success probability of the global attack from 29% to 6.5% and has a ROSI of 10031 EUR.

5 Conclusion

Gadyatskaya et al. [9] have shown how attack–defence trees can be used to model risk reduction engendered by a library of security controls. Since the implementation of defensive mechanisms comes at a cost, it is not *a prori* clear which controls to prefer over which ones. The authors determine the optimal defence strategy by literally processing all combinations of selecting security controls and computing the Return On Security Investment (ROSI) for each of them.

The tool presented in [9], 'ADTop', reaches its feasible limits at 16 defences. However, *any* pure brute-force program would have a practical limit of 40 defences. Indeed, if an evaluation of a single combination takes 1 ms, then iterating over all 2^{40} combinations will already take approximately 13 days (growing exponentially with the number of defences).

This paper improves on the latter work by presenting a memory-efficient algorithm which skips some of the unnecessary computations. This method experimentally decreases the running time of the algorithm on large trees (81 attacks, 90 defences) from several hundred years to several hours. While the technique works specifically for the ROSI function, it can be generalised to other, similar score functions, as well.

The improved algorithm has been applied in a case study in order to highlight the performance boosts. The case study deals with determining the optimal set of ISO 27002 countermeasures that shall be implemented for a pseudonymisation service, and uses an attack–defence tree consisting of 81 attacks and 16 unique defences. Compared to 'ADTop', the new algorithm reduces the memory usage from over 1 GiB to 20 MiB, and the execution time from nearly a minute to less than a second.

Acknowledgements. This work was supported by the Fonds National de la Recherche, Luxembourg (project reference 10239425) and the European Commission's Seventh Framework Programme (FP7/2007-2013) under grant agreement number 318003 (TREsPASS).

References

1. Giannopoulos, G., Filippini, R., Schimmer, M.: Risk Assessment Methodologies for Critical Infrastructure Protection, Part i: A State of the Art. Publications Office of the European Union, Luxembourg (2012)
2. International Organization for Standardization, ISO/IEC 27005 - information technology - security techniques - information security risk management (2011)
3. Bundesamt für Sicherheit in der Informationstechnik (BSI), IT-Grundschutz

4. Amutio, M.A., Candau, J., Mañas, J.: Magerit-version 3, methodology for information systems risk analysis and management, book I - the method, Ministerio de administraciones públicas (2014)
5. Secrétariat général de la défense nationale, Ebios-expression des besoins et identification des objectifs de sécurité (2004)
6. Kordy, B., Mauw, S., Radomirović, S., Schweitzer, P.: Attack–defense trees. J. Logic Comput. **24**(1), 55 (2014). doi:10.1093/logcom/exs029
7. Schneier, B.: Attack trees. Dr. Dobb's J. **24**(12), 21–29 (1999)
8. Kordy, B., Mauw, S., Melissen, M., Schweitzer, P.: Attack–defense trees and two-player binary zero-sum extensive form games are equivalent. In: Alpcan, T., Buttyán, L., Baras, J.S. (eds.) GameSec 2010. LNCS, vol. 6442, pp. 245–256. Springer, Heidelberg (2010). doi:10.1007/978-3-642-17197-0_17
9. Gadyatskaya, O., Harpes, C., Mauw, S., Muller, C., Muller, S.: Bridging two worlds: reconciling practical risk assessment methodologies with theory of attack trees. In: Kordy, B., Ekstedt, M., Kim, D.S. (eds.) GraMSec 2016. LNCS, vol. 9987, pp. 80–93. Springer, Cham (2016). doi:10.1007/978-3-319-46263-9_5
10. International Organization for Standardization, ISO/IEC 27002 - information technology - security techniques - code of practice for information security management (2013)
11. Dewri, R., Poolsappasit, N., Ray, I., Whitley, D.: Optimal security hardening using multi-objective optimization on attack tree models of networks. In: Proceedings of the 14th ACM Conference on Computer and Communications Security, pp. 204–213. ACM (2007)
12. Roy, A., Kim, D.S., Trivedi, K.S.: Scalable optimal countermeasure selection using implicit enumeration on attack countermeasure trees. In: IEEE/IFIP International Conference on Dependable Systems and Networks (DSN 2012), pp. 1–12. IEEE (2012)
13. Kordy, B., Mauw, S., Radomirović, S., Schweitzer, P.: Foundations of attack–defense trees. In: Degano, P., Etalle, S., Guttman, J. (eds.) FAST 2010. LNCS, vol. 6561, pp. 80–95. Springer, Heidelberg (2011). doi:10.1007/978-3-642-19751-2_6
14. Gordon, L.A., Loeb, M.P.: The economics of information security investment. ACM Trans. Inform. Syst. Secur. (TISSEC) **5**(4), 438–457 (2002)
15. Luenberger, D.G.: Introduction to Linear and Nonlinear Programming, vol. 28. Addison-Wesley Reading, MA (1973)

An Assessment of Security Analysis Tools for Cyber-Physical Systems

Laurens Lemaire[(✉)], Jan Vossaert, Bart De Decker, and Vincent Naessens

Department of Computer Science, KU Leuven, IMinds-DistriNet, Leuven, Belgium
{laurens.lemaire,jan.vossaert,bart.dedecker,
vincent.naessens}@cs.kuleuven.be

Abstract. Cyber-Physical Systems are heavily used in today's world. However, their security leaves much to be desired. Attacks such as the Stuxnet worm and the Ukrainian Grid Hack have shown that compromising these systems can have disastrous consequences.

It follows that additional methods for assessing the security of these systems must be explored. To this end, several tools have been developed. In this paper, five existing tools that examine the security of cyber-physical systems are presented. The input models and feedback of these tools are then compared with each other. A real life case study has been modelled in all five tools to achieve this. Two versions of this case study are implemented, one with a DMZ in the network and one without. The five tools are evaluated and their strengths and weaknesses for assessing the security of cyber-physical systems are analysed.

Finally, additional methods for the security assessment are touched upon, and we discuss how they can be used together with the tools.

Keywords: Cyber-physical systems · Security assessment · CSET · ADVISE · CyberSAGE · CySeMoL · FAST-CPS

1 Introduction

Cyber-Physical Systems (CPS) are networks of interacting elements with physical input and output. A CPS usually comprises various remote field sites where a certain process is taking place. Each field site consists of sensors and actuators, controlled locally by a PLC, RTU, or similar device. These remote sites are connected to a centralized control network where operators can remotely monitor and control the processes.

These processes are often of critical nature. Examples of CPS include power stations, nuclear reactors, waste water treatment facilities, wind turbines, traffic lights, and many more. It is easy to see that a failure in any of these systems could have disastrous consequences. Therefore, the security of these systems should be paramount. Unfortunately, most of these systems contain legacy equipment that was not designed with security in mind [10,24].

In the past these CPS were isolated, and the only security concern was physical access to the site. Nowadays, due to the evolution of IT, these systems are

© Springer International Publishing AG 2017
J. Großmann et al. (Eds.): RISK 2016, LNCS 10224, pp. 66–81, 2017.
DOI: 10.1007/978-3-319-57858-3_6

connected to company networks, and by extension the internet. This means they are easier to use, but also easier to attack. As a result, they have been attacked more frequently in the past years. Famous examples include the Maroochy Shire sewage spill in Australia [2], and the Stuxnet worm in Iran [6,16]. The former caused 800.000 L of raw sewage to spill into local parks and rivers, the latter was used to sabotage the fuel enrichment plant of Natanz in Iran [9]. More recently, the Ukrainian grid was hacked which caused hundreds of thousands of people to lose power for several hours [3,27].

It is clear that the security of these systems is not yet sufficient. Tools have been developed to help analyse the security of CPS. This paper will investigate some of them and make a comparison.

1.1   Contribution

This paper presents five tools that help analyse the security of cyber-physical systems. One tool, the Cyber Security Evaluation Tool (CSET), is developed by Homeland Security. The other four tools are the Cyber Security Modeling Language (CySeMoL), the Adversary View Security Evaluation (ADVISE), the Framework for the Analysis of Security in CPS (FAST-CPS), and the Cyber Security Argument Graph Evaluation tool (CyberSAGE). These are developed by research initiatives. To the best of our knowledge, no other CPS security analysis tools exist that can be tested.

All tools are introduced, and then they are used to evaluate a real case study. Their input models are compared to each other, and the feedback they produce is compared as well.

The case study is based on the dam of Nisramont in Belgium. We model this case study with two different architectures, based on the architectures of Figs. 5-1 and 5-3 in the National Institute of Standards and Technology (NIST) Special Publication 800-82 guide [22].

Additional security methodologies are briefly touched upon at the end. The pros and cons of all tools and methods are investigated, and a conclusion is drawn with regards to optimally securing a cyber-physical system.

1.2   Outline

The paper is structured as follows. Section 2 introduces the case study and both architectures. In Sect. 3, the five tools are introduced and used to model both architectures of the case study. In Sect. 4, the tools are compared to each other. Section 5 contains some other methodologies that can be used for the security assessment of CPS. Finally, Sect. 6 concludes the paper.

2   Case Study

In this section we present the case study that will be modelled in the tools. It should be noted that they have different input models, hence not all details of the case study will be modelled in all tools. For instance, process parameters and invariants are only modelled in FAST-CPS.

The case study is based on the dam of Nisramont in Belgium. The industrial process in Nisramont monitors the water level of a lake and keeps it constant. A sensor is used to measure the water level, and this info is passed on to a Schneider Electric PLC of type Premium. An industrial PC with the Vijeo Citect SCADA package is used locally to monitor the process. The control network is connected with the offices in Verviers from where remote control is possible. The process data is also stored in the data historian located in these offices. A data historian is an application that logs time-based process data.

We model two different architectures in each tool, based on the architectures of Figs. 5-1 and 5-3 in the NIST SP 800-82 guide [22]. The first architecture only contains the two network zones described above: the control network and the corporate network. The second architecture adds a DMZ between these two network zones where the historian is located. We will test whether the tools produce different results in these different architectures.

Some tools model the users in the system. We will include one operator who has access to the control network, and one employee who works in the Verviers office. There will also be an outside attacker. In case studies where attacker goals have to be specified, the attacker will attempt to gain access to the data historian.

3   Tools

Here the five tools are introduced, and their input model and feedback are discussed when modelling the case study.

3.1   CSET

Homeland Security has created CSET, the Cyber Security Evaluation Tool [8]. This tool checks compliance of a system with a chosen standard through a question and answer method. There are 24 standards the user can choose between. Once a standard has been chosen, the tool generates a list of questions that will assess system compliance with the given standard.

CSET also has a diagram feature where the user can model the network topology of their system. The tool then gives warnings in order to assist the user in finding a better network architecture. From this diagram, the user can also generate a list of questions from a standard, but only questions related to the components in the system. Hence this feature helps in condensing the big list of questions.

Both architectures of the case study were implemented in CSET. The input model of this tool focuses mainly on network architecture. Process information, users, and attackers cannot be modelled. It is also not possible to add properties of components or communication channels. The feedback of both architectures

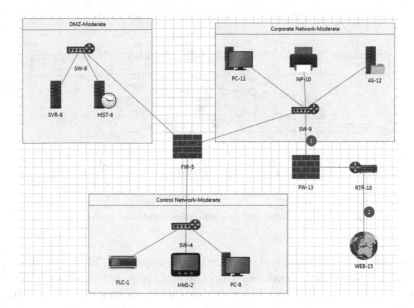

Fig. 1. The DMZ architecture modelled in CSET

was the same, the inclusion of a DMZ did not change anything. The tool displayed 2 warnings, as can be seen in Fig. 1. Warning 1 said that the corporate network should have an IDS or IPS in-line to confirm that the firewall FW-13 is configured correctly, and warning 2 recommends the use of yet another firewall as there is a connection on one side to an external network.

CSET is easy to use and it has by far the most components in its panel, allowing you to accurately model your system. Unfortunately the feedback is lacking, the main aim of the tool is to facilitate compliance with standards, not assessing the security of a system.

3.2 ADVISE

ADVISE [13] determines which way an attacker is most likely to go about attacking a system. The tool has been added to the Möbius framework [7] to make use of its modelling formalisms and solution techniques.

Modelling the case study in ADVISE is done from the point of view of the attacker. First the user must decide what the attacker goals are. For instance, in this case study there could be five different attacker goals: Reading the data from the historian, corrupting the data from the historian, changing PLC instructions, forwarding unauthorized PLC code, and compromising the control server. Next, the user adds the *attack steps* that the attacker must complete before the goals are reached. For example, to reach the *read data* goal node, the attacker must perform the attack step *Access Data Historian*.

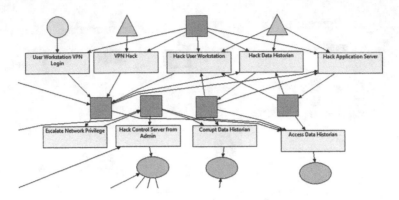

Fig. 2. Attack steps and prerequisites modelled in ADVISE

Each attack step is then assigned further prerequisites. There are three possible types: *access* to networks or workstations, required attacker *skills*, and *knowledge* such as passwords. The result of an attack step can be an attacker goal, or increased access/knowledge for the attacker. For instance, prerequisites of the *Access Data Historian* step could be *Application Server Access*, *Data Historian Access*, etc. The attack steps resulting in these access rights are *Hack Application Server*, and *Hack Data Historian*, and the prerequisites for these involve certain attacker skills. Part of the input for our case study is shown in Fig. 2. Circles denote knowledge, squares are access, and triangles are skills. The ovals are the goal nodes.

When the user has mapped out all the attack steps, he now has to model the adversary. This includes specifying the attacker's initial knowledge/access and the attacker proficiency in all skills. The user also indicates how much the attacker cares about detection versus pay-off, and the relative importance of the different goals.

The result is an Attack Execution Graph (AEG). The AEG represents potential attack steps against the system. ADVISE automatically generates an executable model that represents how the adversary is likely to attack the system. Once the attack execution graph is modelled, the user can run the framework to determine which attacker goals will be reached with what probability. It is also shown how many time steps the attacker will need to reach his goal. This type of model-based security analysis distinguishes itself from attack trees in the fact that it allows for time-ordered sequences of events. Attack trees do not contain a notion of time. Other system security analysis techniques exist that employ adversary-based analysis. For instance MORDA [5] and NRAT [25]. However, neither of these is designed for state-based analysis. The adversary attack decision represented in these methods is a one-time selection of a full attack path. In contrast, ADVISE models step-by-step decisions, in which the outcome of previous attack step decisions impacts the adversary's subsequent decisions.

For the case study, two different attack execution graphs were modelled. The DMZ architecture adds an extra access domain (the DMZ), and two additional attack steps. Several attackers were modelled, with different preferences towards detection and goals. A highly-skilled adversary, who cared more about reaching the goal rather than remaining undetected, was able to eventually read the data with probability 1. In the DMZ architecture, this took more time steps to accomplish, but otherwise there were no differences. Changing the pay-off of the attack goals resulted in other attacks succeeding. If the detection preference weight was increased accordingly, no attacker goals were reached.

To use ADVISE, the user requires quite a bit of security knowledge. Building the attack execution graph from scratch is not trivial. The user must know how an attacker would go about breaching their network beforehand. The attacker also has to be given certain properties, such as his skill level at exploiting VPNs, hacking control servers through an HMI, hacking data historians, etc. Assigning accurate values to these skills is hard to do. Furthermore, each attack step needs to be given a percentage chance of detection. Finding the "correct" values for these probabilities is not possible, hence a big part of the attack execution graph works on assumptions.

3.3   CyberSAGE

CyberSAGE [23] is similar to ADVISE in terms of output. The user will have to specify a workflow of the threat agent, and the result will show probabilities of the attacker reaching his goal and his attack steps. However, the tool is easier to use as the attack steps are fixed and there are less attacker variables to decide on.

To generate the resulting argument graph, the user needs to provide four pieces of input. First there is the workflow graph which specifies the actions of the attacker. There is a list of 19 possible actions the user can choose from, including *send command, physical access, inject malicious messages*, and so on. The user has the possibility to add additional actions in the rules engine. An example workflow of a threat agent who attempts to gain access to a historian is shown in Fig. 3.

Next, the user models the system components and networks. This is largely similar to the diagram feature of CSET, with the exception that components can have various properties regarding authentication, access control, encryption, etc. Less components are available, but the user can add his own components and properties to the palette.

Finally, the user must model the attacker. The attacker attributes include his skills, his intention, his access to the system, and his resources. There are less parameters than in ADVISE, but this is not necessarily a bad thing, the essentials are there.

The final element of input is the rules engine. A default rules file is supplied with each CyberSAGE instance. The user has the option to edit this and tweak with the probabilities, or add additional attacker actions.

Both architectures of the test case were modelled, and it was tested whether two attackers were able to read the data in the historian: an insider and an

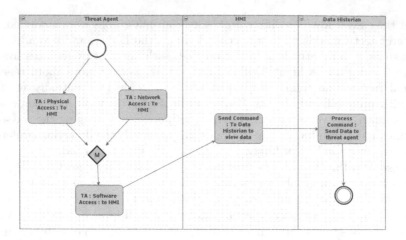

Fig. 3. A workflow modelled in CyberSAGE

outsider with the same level of IT skills. As expected, the insider could access the data of the historian with probability 1 in both architectures. This is due to the fact that the insider has physical and logical access. Interestingly, the outsider has the same probability of reading the data in both architectures: 0.897. The DMZ does not appear to change the outcome. When changing all the component properties of the firewall between the corporate network and the DMZ, the probability does not change. CyberSAGE is still under development, perhaps the component properties do not yet affect the probability.

CyberSAGE is easier to work with than ADVISE. Less security knowledge is required, and the user does not have to define the probabilities of detection for each step. The tool is fully customizable to suit the user's needs. Properties of the components in the system diagram do not seem to affect the outcome yet.

3.4 CySeMoL

CySeMoL [20,21] provides the same kind of feedback as the two previous tools, e.g. the probability of an attacker reaching some attack goals in a system. However, in CySeMoL both the attacker and the attacker goals are fixed, the user cannot change them. For their attack probabilities, CySeMoL assumes that the attacker is a penetration tester who only has access to public tools.

Using CySeMoL does not require security expertise from the user. He just has to model his system according to the Probabilistic Relational Model (PRM) employed by CySeMoL. The PRM specifies a theory on how attributes in the model depend on each other. The theory used in CySeMoL is based on logical relations, experimental research in the security domain, and domain experts' judgement.

A PRM can be used to perform two types of analysis. The first method can produce values for the expected economic losses for the architecture. This analysis considers the probability that different attack scenarios will be attempted and the expected loss if they succeed. A second method uses a subset of the PRM template and calculates reachability values for different attack paths, as in attack graphs. CySeMoL uses the second type of analysis.

Compared to other tools that employ methods based on attack graphs, such as NETSPA [14,15], MulVAL [18], or the TVA-tool [17], CySeMoL analyses a wider range of attack types and security measures. For instance, it has the capability to model attacks such as password cracking, social engineering, and DoS attacks, which the other tools do not.

When modelling the network architecture, the available components on the palette do not include typical CPS components, but rather a general *OperatingSystem* block that can be used for all PLCs, HMIs, and so on. These can then be connected with the relevant *ApplicationServer* or *ApplicationClient* components. Each component has a fixed number of attributes linked to it, for instance the *ApplicationClient* component has an attribute *HasAllPatches* which the user can change to false or true. Modelling a CPS in CySeMoL is not as straightforward as with the other tools, but there are several tutorials available.

When modelling the case study in CySeMoL, the attacker was given direct access to his own PC, an *OperatingSystem* object, which was connected to the internet. The internet is connected to the corporate network, which is connected to the control network. Both networks are then modelled in more detail than the previous tools, including software of components, users, social zones, data flows, and more. Firewalls separate all networks. When calculating the probabilities, the attacker can access the corporate network with probability 0.02 and the control network and DMZ with probability 0.0. Hence in the first architecture he can access the data historian with probability 0.02, and in the second architecture he cannot access it.

CySeMoL only considers one type of attacker, which decreases its applicability. Compared to ADVISE and CyberSAGE, the returned probability of gaining access to the data historian is very different, the lack of attacker customization may be a cause. The advantage is that the user needs no security expertise to use CySeMoL, only the system has to be modelled, much like CSET. For experienced users, the Class Modeller can be downloaded to change CySeMoL's metamodel and configure the probabilities and default properties of components. The research group that worked on CySeMoL is currently working on a successor where the user will be able to choose between attackers of various strength.

3.5   FAST-CPS

FAST-CPS [11,12] provides a different kind of feedback than the other tools. Here the user will model the entire system in the UML-based visual modeling language SysML. This includes information about the process, the system, the users, the products, and the attacker. IDP3, a logic-based framework [4,26], will then report vulnerabilities in the system model. The logic theory which will find these vulnerabilities is based on component vulnerability databases, the Scadastrangelove Github [1] containing CPS components with known default passwords, and security best practices extracted from various standards, guidelines, and academic papers.

The feedback of FAST-CPS is twofold. First the components with known component vulnerabilities or known default passwords will be listed. Then the logic will evaluate a set of queries related to the normal behaviour of the system and let the user know whether this is impacted. For instance, the user must model a permission matrix showing which users should be able to perform certain operations on parameters. If the component vulnerabilities result in additional or fewer permissions, these will be reported as system vulnerabilities.

When modelling the case studies in FAST-CPS, both architectures yield the same component vulnerabilities. The Schneider Electric Premium PLC is listed on the Scadastrangelove Github, meaning anyone can authenticate himself to the PLC if the factory passwords have not been changed. Furthermore, the Vijeo Citect Historian and HMI are both listed in the ICS CERT vulnerability database. The historian is vulnerable to a buffer overflow, which could cause a DoS, while an attacker with access to the HMI could abuse XML entities with URLs to gain access to confidential data. The latter two vulnerabilities have patches available that can fix them.

In terms of system vulnerabilities, both architectures report that users may not be able to read the historian, despite having permission to do so, as a result of the buffer overflow vulnerability. No differences exist between both architectures in terms of feedback.

In order to use FAST-CPS, a user does not need extensive knowledge of CPS security. The process is mostly automated, the only steps to take are to create a complete inventory of the system, and then to model it. To create this inventory, a scanning tool such as CyberLens could be used, or the operator could consult blueprints or other resources. Afterwards, the tool can be run and the user no longer has to interfere. The feedback differs from other tools, listing component vulnerabilities that are present in the system and the system vulnerabilities they may cause. There are no probabilities involved. As such, the attacker model is less detailed than the one in ADVISE and CyberSAGE, no attacker skills or goals are modelled.

4   Comparison of Tools

In this section we will compare the different tools with each other. We first consider the input model and then the feedback the tools return.

4.1   Input Model

Here we compare which parts of a cyber-physical system are modelled in the different tools. We also include whether the tools have customizable rules and whether the user is assumed to have security expertise. A general overview can be found in Table 1. All tools except ADVISE require the user to model the system. Which elements of the system are modelled differ from tool to tool,

Table 1. Input model comparison.

Tool	System model	Attacker model	Customisable rules	Security expertise
CSET	X			
ADVISE		X		X
CyberSAGE	X	X	X	X
CySeMoL	X		X	
FAST-CPS	X	X	X	

this is examined in the next paragraph. Similarly, the final table in this subsection shows the attacker info that is modelled in the different tools. CSET does not include an attacker, and in CySeMoL the attacker is predetermined and the user does not have to change his properties. CyberSAGE, CySeMoL, and FAST-CPS can be customized. The former two have fixed probabilities attached to certain properties, the user can edit these to their liking. In FAST-CPS, the user can add component vulnerabilities as new ones appear on the ICS CERT or Scadastrangelove listings. Finally, only ADVISE and CyberSAGE require security expertise from the user. In both tools, the user must construct a workflow for the attacker. Hence the user should be aware how an attacker is most likely going to attack their system.

Table 2. System model comparison.

Tool	Components & channels	Data flow	Users	Process	Software
CSET	X				
CyberSAGE	X				
CySeMoL	X	X	X		X
FAST-CPS	X	X	X	X	X

Table 2 shows which elements of the system that are modelled in the four tools that require a system model as input. All tools include a list of components and the communication channels between them. CySeMoL and FAST-CPS attach further properties to these channels, for instance the data flow that comes through them, the protocols that are used, etc. Both in CySeMoL and FAST-CPS, the users of the system are modelled too, albeit for different purposes. In CySeMoL, a modeller can place the attacker in the same social zone as a legitimate user, in which case the risk of social engineering increases. In FAST-CPS, the system also investigates whether regular users can carry out their tasks when certain component or system vulnerabilities are present. Process information is only required for FAST-CPS. This includes process invariants, parameters, sensors and actuators. The system will check whether the parameters can only be

Table 3. Attacker model comparison.

Tool	Knowledge	Access	Skills	Goal	Considerations
ADVISE	X	X	X	X	X
CyberSAGE		X	X	X	
FAST-CPS	X	X			

read by the users who are authorized to do so, and whether the process invariants can be abused to modify certain parameters. Finally, the software of the components is modelled in CySeMoL and FAST-CPS only. This includes operating systems of workstations, authentication info of programs, etc.

Table 3 compares the three tools that require an attacker to be modelled. ADVISE and FAST-CPS consider the knowledge of the attacker, meaning passwords and other login tokens the attacker might possess. All three tools consider the access level of the attacker, but they do this in different ways. CyberSAGE asks whether the attacker has physical or logical access to the system as a whole. FAST-CPS has the user specify components the attacker has physical access to, network access is inferred from this info and the attacker knowledge. ADVISE can have access as a prerequisite or a result of an attack step, the attacker is given an initial set of access variables. The attacker skills are modelled in ADVISE and CyberSAGE, they help compute the probability of success of certain actions. In CyberSAGE, the user must choose between low/medium/high, in ADVISE an actual value between 0 and 1000 must be assigned. Both tools also contain the attacker goals, it is the probability of reaching this goal that will be computed. FAST-CPS does not include attacker skills or goals. Finally, ADVISE takes additional factors in consideration such as the attacker's priorities: does he care more about remaining undetected, cost of the attack, or achieving goals with high pay-off? As a result, detection rates, attack step costs, and goal pay-off must also be modelled.

4.2 Feedback

The feedback of the tools was already largely touched upon in Sect. 3, we will summarise it here. CSET's diagram feature aims to assist users with their network architecture. The feedback focuses on firewall placement, network zones, intrusion detection systems, internet access points, etc. It will alert the user to possible vulnerabilities in their architecture. This is quite limited, combining it with one of the other tools is advised.

ADVISE, CyberSAGE and CySeMoL all return the probability of an attacker reaching some goal. In the former two, the attackers and the goals can be customized, in CySeMoL these are both fixed. CySeMoL's feedback is mainly centred around reachability of components in the network. ADVISE and Cyber-SAGE can contain a larger variety of attacker goals. What's interesting is that these tools gave a very different percentage chance for the attacker to access the data historian. In ADVISE, the probability was 1 for both architectures, in CyberSAGE it was 0.897 for both architectures, and in CySeMoL it was 0 for the DMZ architecture and 0.02 for the other. This is due to a combination of reasons. First of all, we modelled a skilful attacker in both ADVISE and Cyber-SAGE, while the skills of the attacker are predetermined in CySeMoL. Perhaps the attacker is modelled too weak. Secondly, the system model in CySeMoL was more in-depth, including firewalls, operating systems, software, authentication, etc. In ADVISE, there is no system model, and in CyberSAGE it is still quite basic. Changing the properties of components in the CyberSAGE system model also did not have an effect on the final probability. Presumably the probability of an attacker actually breaching the historian in the DMZ is somewhere between 0.897 and 0, and the feedback of these tools must be taken with a grain of salt.

FAST-CPS returns the component vulnerabilities in the CPS, and the resulting system vulnerabilities they may cause. This is feedback that the previous three tools do not provide, hence it could be used together with one of them. FAST-CPS could first identify component vulnerabilities, these could then be taken into account when modelling the attacker workflow or system properties in order to get a more accurate probability of attack.

Table 4. Runtime comparison. The given number is the average of fifty timed runs. The measurements were performed on a Dell Latitude E6530 with an Intel Core i7-3740QM CPU at 2.7 GHz

	ADVISE	CyberSAGE	CySeMoL	FAST-CPS
Runtime	19.56s	5.63s	11.12s	3.36s

Finally, Table 4 contains a runtime comparison of four tools. Feedback of CSET appears instantaneously when adding new elements to a system diagram, hence it is not included. The other tools finish fairly quick. The case study was of a fully functional system with corporate network included. Of course, it is possible to have much larger systems with hundreds of remote field sites. Whether the tools would still finish in reasonable time then remains to be tested.

5   Other Methods for Security Assessment

There are other ways to analyse the security of cyber-physical systems, they will be discussed here and briefly contrasted with the tools.

5.1   Audits

A popular way of assessing the security of a system is to perform a security audit. An audit can be performed on two levels: high-level risk assessment, and low-level technical assessment. When performing a technical assessment, one of the first steps is to create an inventory of the customer's environment (should this be non existing), or in case there is one provided, check whether the current inventory is correct and complete. Tools like nessus, nmap, CyberLens or network monitoring tools can help here. Once established, the components of the inventory are sometimes assigned a criticality level. Then, various technical scans can be used against these components to verify their vulnerability and security level. These can include penetration tests, intrusion tests, scans, etc. Whilst doing these, the assessor assumes the role of an attacker. Both external and internal attackers can be considered, as well as disgruntled employees. Tests are not only logical in nature, the assessor can also go on site to verify the physical access of the system and environment. During this physical walk-through, the inventory will be completed with missing information and/or systems.

A downside of security audits is that they offer a one-time snapshot of the CPS security. Security should be a continuous process. If new vulnerabilities are discovered, or components are changed, the system should be re-evaluated. With the tools, this is easy to do, with an audit not so much.

However, auditors can offer excellent feedback on how to improve system security. This is one of the biggest advantages over the tools, which only help to identify issues, but do not offer solutions. Audits are performed by security experts who can immediately suggest improvements or fixes.

5.2　Standards and Guidelines

Another alternative is to use standards and guidelines and analyse the security of the system yourself. A first issue here is to choose which standard your system will comply with. In most European countries, there are no compliance regulations yet and the user can choose between dozens of standards. In North America, systems in the energy sector have to comply with the NERC CIP standard. Penalties for non-compliance vary from country to country, but can include fines, sanctions, or other actions against covered entities.

A second point is that the standards are not always optimal. A paper by Schlegel et al. investigates the security of the IEC 62351 standard [19], and finds a few guidelines that they disagree with. Standards and guidelines also do not look at component vulnerabilities.

Finally, going through a standard that is hundreds of pages long will take some time, and requires some security knowledge from the reader. However, this is where CSET can come in handy. If the chosen standard is part of CSET, the tool will check compliance of the system with the chosen standard through a question and answer method. At the end of the evaluation, it will display which recommendations of the standard that the system did not comply with, but it will not offer solutions.

5.3　Intrusion Detection/Prevention Systems

A final security measure we will consider in this paper is Intrusion Detection/Prevention Systems (IDS/IPS). These systems identify malicious activity, log information about this activity, attempt to block/stop it, and report it. A distinction can be made between host based and network based intrusion detection systems (HIDS/NIDS). It should be noted that these systems can not always be deployed on industrial networks due to the high availability requirements.

Various intrusion detection methods exist. Blacklisting, also called signature detection, is often used. It works by having a collection of attack signatures and scanning the network to see if these signatures are found, and then taking the appropriate action. The opposite approach is white listing, where only certain protocols or applications are allowed, and all other traffic is blocked. Anomaly detection is somewhat less strict, aiming to determine the normal network activity and acting when unusual activity takes place. These latter two methods are the only way to stop zero-day attacks. Hence it is always recommended to run an IDS/IPS on your system in combination with other security analysis measures.

6 Conclusion

This paper compares five security analysis tools for cyber-physical systems. The tools are CSET, ADVISE, CyberSAGE, CySeMoL and FAST-CPS. The five tools are used to evaluate the security of a case study: the Nisramont dam in Belgium. The input models and the feedback of the tools are compared to each other, and also with other security assessment methodologies. For both the input model and the feedback, there are fairly big differences between the tools, but no tool comes out superior to the others. In order to adequately protect the security of your system, a combination of tools and methodologies is advised.

6.1 Future Work

Three tools return the probability of an attacker reaching attack goals. In our case study, the returned probabilities for a specific attack vary wildly between the tools. Further investigation is required to understand why this is the case. An overall strategy for securing CPS which combines the presented tools and methodologies in this paper will be developed.

Acknowledgements. Research funded by a PhD grant of the Agency for Innovation by Science and Technology in Flanders (IWT).

The CyberSAGE software, used by the authors, was developed by the "Integrative Security Assessment of Smart Grid Cyber Infrastructure" project, and is jointly owned by the Illinois Pte ADSC and The Agency for Science Technology and Research in Singapore.

References

1. Hardcoded passwords list (2016). https://github.com/scadastrangelove/SCADA PASS/blob/master/scadapass.csv
2. Abrams, M., Weiss, J.: Malicious control system cyber security attack case study-maroochy water services, Australia (2008)

3. Assante, M.: Confirmation of a coordinated attack on the Ukrainian power grid (2016). https://ics.sans.org/blog/2016/01/09/confirmation-of-a-coordinated-attack-on-the-ukrainian-power-grid

4. Bogaerts, B., De Cat, B., De Pooter, S., Denecker, M.: The IDP framework reference manual (2012)

5. Evans, S., Wallner, J.: Risk-based security engineering through the eyes of the adversary. In: Proceedings from the Sixth Annual IEEE SMC Information Assurance Workshop, IAW 2005, pp. 158–165. IEEE (2005)

6. Falliere, N., Murchu, L., Chien, E.: W32.Stuxnet Dossier (2011). http://www.symantec.com/content/en/us/enterprise/media/security_response/whitepapers/w32_stuxnet_dossier.pdf

7. Ford, M.D., Keefe, K., LeMay, E., Sanders, W.H., Muehrcke, C.: Implementing the advise security modeling formalism in möbius. In: 2013 43rd Annual IEEE/IFIP International Conference on Dependable Systems and Networks (DSN), pp. 1–8. IEEE (2013)

8. Homeland Security, H.C.C.: Cset: Cyber security evaluation tool (2014)

9. Langner, R.: To kill a centrifuge: a technical analysis of what stuxnet's creators tried to achieve (2013)

10. Lee, E.A.: Cyber physical systems: design challenges. In: 2008 11th IEEE International Symposium on Object Oriented Real-Time Distributed Computing (ISORC), pp. 363–369. IEEE (2008)

11. Lemaire, L., Lapon, J., De Decker, B., Naessens, V.: A SysML extension for security analysis of industrial control systems. In: Proceedings of the 2nd International Symposium for ICS & SCADA Cyber Security Research, p. 1 (2014)

12. Lemaire, L., Vossaert, J., Jansen, J., Naessens, V.: Extracting vulnerabilities in industrial control systems using a knowledge-based system. In: Proceedings of the 3rd International Symposium for ICS & SCADA Cyber Security Research, p. 1 (2015)

13. LeMay, E., Ford, M.D., Keefe, K., Sanders, W.H., Muehrcke, C.: Model-based security metrics using adversary view security evaluation (advise). In: 2011 Eighth International Conference on Quantitative Evaluation of Systems (QEST), pp. 191–200. IEEE (2011)

14. Lippmann, R., Ingols, K., Scott, C., Piwowarski, K., Kratkiewicz, K., Artz, M., Cunningham, R.: Validating and restoring defense in depth using attack graphs. In: IEEE Military Communications Conference, MILCOM 2006, pp. 1–10. IEEE (2006)

15. Lippmann, R., Scott, C., Kratkiewicz, K., Artz, M., Ingols, K.W.: Network security planning architecture. US Patent 7,194,769, 20 March 2007

16. Matrosov, A., Researcher, S.V., Rodionov, E., Analyst, R., Harley, D.: Stuxnet Under the Microscope (2011)

17. Noel, S., Elder, M., Jajodia, S., Kalapa, P., O'Hare, S., Prole, K.: Advances in topological vulnerability analysis. In: Cybersecurity Applications & Technology Conference For Homeland Security, CATCH 2009, pp. 124–129. IEEE (2009)

18. Ou, X., Govindavajhala, S., Appel, A.W.: Mulval: A logic-based network security analyzer. In: USENIX security (2005)

19. Schlegel, R., Obermeier, S., Schneider, J.: Assessing the security of IEC 62351. In: Proceedings of the 3rd International Symposium for ICS & SCADA Cyber Security Research, pp. 11–19. British Computer Society (2015)

20. Sommestad, T., Ekstedt, M., Holm, H.: The cyber security modeling language: a tool for assessing the vulnerability of enterprise system architectures. IEEE Syst. J. **7**(3), 363–373 (2013)

21. Sommestad, T., Ekstedt, M., Nordström, L.: A case study applying the cyber security modeling language (2010)
22. Stouffer, K., Lightman, S., Pillitteri, V., Abrams, M., Hahn, A.: Guide to industrial control systems (ICS) security (2015)
23. Vu, A.H., Tippenhauer, N.O., Chen, B., Nicol, D.M., Kalbarczyk, Z.: CyberSAGE: a tool for automatic security assessment of cyber-physical systems. In: Norman, G., Sanders, W. (eds.) QEST 2014. LNCS, vol. 8657, pp. 384–387. Springer, Cham (2014). doi:10.1007/978-3-319-10696-0_29
24. Wang, E.K., Ye, Y., Xu, X., Yiu, S., Hui, L., Chow, K.: Security issues and challenges for cyber physical system. In: Proceedings of the 2010 IEEE/ACM International Conference on Green Computing and Communications & International Conference on Cyber, Physical and Social Computing, pp. 733–738. IEEE Computer Society (2010)
25. Whiteman, B.: Network risk assessment tool (NRAT). IA Newsl. 11(1), 4–8 (2008)
26. Wittocx, J., Mariën, M., Denecker, M.: The IDP system: a model expansion system for an extension of classical logic. In: Proceedings of the 2nd Workshop on Logic and Search, pp. 153–165 (2008)
27. Zetter, K.: Inside the cunning, unprecedented hack of Ukraine's power grid (2016). http://www.wired.com/2016/03/inside-cunning-unprecedented-hack-ukraines-power-grid/

Supporting Risk Assessment with the Systematic Identification, Merging, and Validation of Security Goals

Daniel Angermeier[✉], Alexander Nieding, and Jörn Eichler

Fraunhofer AISEC, Garching near Munich, Germany
{daniel.angermeier,alexander.nieding,joern.eichler}@aisec.fraunhofer.de

Abstract. Assessing security-related risks in software or systems engineering is a challenging task: often, a heterogeneous set of distributed stakeholders creates a complex system of (software) components which are highly connected to each other, consumer electronics, or Internet-based services. Changes during development are frequent and must be evaluated and handled efficiently. Consequently, risk assessment itself becomes a complex task and its results must be comprehensible by all actors in the distributed environment. Especially, systematic and repeatable identification of security goals based on a model of the system under development (SUD) is not well-supported in established methods. Thus, we demonstrate how the systematic identification, merging, and validation of security goals based on a model of the SUD in a concrete implementation of our method Modular Risk Assessment (MoRA) supports security engineers to handle this challenge.

Keywords: Risk assessment · Security goals · Model-based · Security engineering · Method

1 Introduction

In software and systems engineering, security risk assessment determines the quality of security risk management for a system under development (SUD) and thus the SUD's protection against threat actors. However, security risk assessment is a challenging task: Modern software is often developed by a heterogeneous set of distributed stakeholders and many of the resulting systems consist of several devices or software components which are highly connected to each other, consumer electronics, or Internet-based services. Frequently changing requirements during development increase the complexity even further and must be evaluated and handled efficiently with respect to limited resources. Consequently, security risk assessment also constitutes a complex task. The resulting work products must be comprehensible by all stakeholders in the distributed environment to facilitate risk management, including the correct design and implementation of security controls. Identification of protection needs for the

J. Großmann et al. (Eds.): RISK 2016, LNCS 10224, pp. 82–95, 2017.
DOI: 10.1007/978-3-319-57858-3_7

assets of an SUD is one of the key challenges within the application of any security risk assessment method and vital to the validity and comprehensibility of
the results. Considering frequent changes the systematic and repeatable determination of protection needs have to complemented by complementary thoughts
for their evolution. Hence, systematic procedures for merging and validation of
protection needs are of high interest.

We developed the method Modular Risk Assessment (MoRA) [6] to tackle
these challenges. Our method features a modular structure, supports a unified
method framework, well-defined work products as interfaces between activities,
and different guidelines as well as catalogs to implement the method in a specific domain and environment. MoRA determines the protection needs based
on *security goals*, represented by the combination of a *security goal class* (e.g.,
confidentiality, integrity, availability) with an asset of the SUD (e.g., confidentiality of the asset "patient data" in the context of a medical system). In this
publication, we present procedures on how to systematically determine, merge,
and validate security goals and thus protection needs for an SUD. These procedures are integrated as guidelines in MoRA. As a running example, we will use
a health care system in which (authenticated) practitioners can query relevant
patient data (e.g., blood types, allergies) from a cluster of database servers.

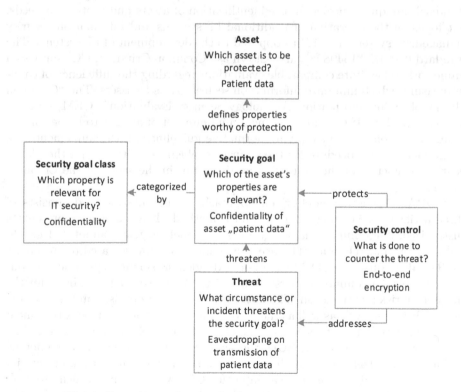

Fig. 1. Overview and examples for security engineering terms

To support a consistent terminology Fig. 1 illustrates key terms for this publication and their relations to each other. The terms are depicted in rectangular boxes, along with an example for each term at the bottom of each box.

The remainder of this publication is structured as follows: In Sect. 2, we elaborate on related work. Section 3 provides a short summary of our method MoRA as background for this publication. A description of the aforementioned guidelines supporting the systematic identification, merging, and validation of protection needs based on a hierarchical model of the SUD follows in Sect. 4. We conclude in Sect. 5.

2   Related Work

Several standards and publications for the assessment and the management of information security risks exist. ISO 31000 [9] in combination with ISO 27005 [10] form a framework for the management of risks with a focus on information security. However, these standards do not explicate guidelines for the identification of important work products, such as security goals and threats. The standards BSI 100-1 [2], BSI 100-2 [3], and 100-3 [4] by the German Federal Office for Information Security provide a baseline protection approach for IT systems. These standards are quite specific on the identification of assets and protection needs, but focus on the operation of traditional IT systems and information security management systems (ISMS) as opposed to the development of IT systems. The standard ISO/IEC 15408 [8] (also known as "Common Criteria", CC) supplies a framework to facilitate comparable evaluations regarding the sufficiency of countermeasures which minimize information security risks to assets. The "Common Methodology for Information Technology Security Evaluation" (CEM) [1] complements the ISO/IEC 15408 defining a minimum set of actions to be performed in an evaluation. While supplying normative guidelines on the implementation of the method, a procedure for the security problem definition (e.g., the identification of assets and the protection needs) is not in the scope of the Common Criteria.

CORAS [12] is a model-driven approach to risk analysis and consists of three artifacts: a language, a tool, and a method. The language represents a customized, diagrammatic language for risk modeling, using annotated graphical symbols and relations. The accompanying tool provides a editor to create CORAS diagrams. The CORAS method is divided into eight steps. The first four steps establish a common understanding of the SUD, serving as a basis for the subsequent risk identification. The identification of concrete risks and the estimation of their risk levels as well as the determination of appropriate risk treatment is the subject of the last four steps. The identification of assets takes place in a customer presentation of the SUD: the scope and assumptions are documented and assets are identified using diagrams such as class, collaboration, or activity diagrams. These diagrams serve as input for CORAS diagrams, which are completed by adding possible threats and risks. Although this approach unites the knowledge of the application and security domain in a customer presentation, no systematic and repeatable procedure for the identification of protection needs is provided.

Islam et al. [7] adopt the results of the HEAVENS project to establish a risk assessment framework for automotive embedded systems. The workflow of the proposed framework is defined by its core activities: At first, the relevant parts of the system under evaluation are defined using system models and data flow diagrams. Using this model, the identified architectural and data elements are then combined with each of the threat categories of the "STRIDE approach to threat modeling" [11,18]. As a result, the framework provides a list of assets and associated threats, each of the threats threatening one or several security goal classes (e.g., integrity). The following risk assessment process supports the prioritization of those threats. By combining the estimate of a threat's likelihood of occurrence ("threat level") and the expected loss of a realized threat ("impact level"), the "security level" is determined. This approach may however lead to redundancy, as each asset/threat pair is estimated individually and relationships between security goals or threats are not explicitly covered. As a result, maintaining consistency of the estimations might be challenging.

Another well-known approach to risk assessment is MITRE's approach "Threat Assessment & Remediation Analysis" (TARA) [22]. TARA focuses on the identification, estimation and scoring of risks and countermeasures in IT systems. TARA can optionally use the output of other methods to determine protection needs, but does not systematically identify assets itself. Therefore, the TARA approach can be used to identify and estimate threats on security goals identified by methods like the one presented in this paper.

As another example, Weldemariam et al. [21] propose a methodological approach to procedural security analysis. After building and reasoning on an extended system model, possible attacks are identified and related to affected assets and their properties (e.g., their value to the organization), analyzed, and evaluated to produce sets of security requirements, which establish a certain level of protection. This approach however features a high grade of formalism regarding the documentation of assets and threats and is, consequently, very demanding in terms of depth of analysis and respective effort.

With concern to security requirements elicitation, Souag et al. developed a generic security ontology [19]. By evaluating the ontology in comparison to existing security ontologies used in security requirements engineering, the authors aim to establish an ontology as complete as possible. The introduced concepts and their relations are similar to those of MoRA, especially "security criteria" can be compared to MoRA's security goals. In combination with axioms and attributes, concepts and relations are used to store knowledge in a formal way. A query language (SQWRL [16]) uses predefined rules to reason on the knowledge base and guides the requirements engineer through the security requirement elicitation process. No functions for the systematic identification, merge, or validation of security criteria are given, but the formal representation of the ontology provides a suitable source for further development of such rules.

A few publications and surveys compare methods which focus on or contain security requirements engineering. Tondel et al. [20] as well as Salini and Kanmani [17] note, that not every approach incorporates steps to validate (intermediate) results. Additionally, a lack of standardized validation methods is identified. Combining the results of the surveys and the previously introduced standards, methods, and frameworks it can be noted, that a number of approaches support the identification of security goals (or similar concepts, e.g. "security criteria" (SQUARE [13]), "security objectives" (Mellado et al. [14]), or "security constraints" (Secure Tropos) [15]) but in general do not define systematic guidelines regarding the identification, merge or validation of security goals, or only employ a generic approach for validation.

3   Background: Modular Risk Assessment

MoRA features four core activities in its *method framework*: "Document SUD", "Determine Protection Needs", "Analyze Threats", and "Analyze Risks", each supported by a set of *guidelines* and *domain-specific preparative work products*. These work products are created in preparative activities for MoRA's application in a specific domain. MoRA relies on an *assessment model* and a set of *catalogs* to homogenize assessments within the domain of application. Thus, the assessment model and the catalogs represent a common basic understanding of all stakeholders regarding critical aspects of risk assessment. In the following, we present an instantiation of our method, which has been successfully applied in practice, as described in [6].

An assessment model contains means and parameters how to estimate impacts of violations of security goals as well as required attack potentials to execute attacks or to overcome security controls. For example, to support impact estimation, a list of damage criteria maps potential damages (e.g., "loss of 10.000 – 50.000 $") to damage potentials (e.g., "moderate"). This helps focus impact estimation on domain facts ("is the damage between 10.000 and 50.000 $?") instead of personal opinions ("I think the damage is moderate"). This particular approach is inspired by the standard BSI 100-2. The aforementioned catalogs entail generalized but pre-evaluated elements used in the method, such as threats and controls. Their purpose is to aid the analyst in the process of determining what to protect, how to attack the elements in need of protection and how to protect the SUD against it.

The activity *Document SUD* provides the basis for MoRA's approach, where security engineers and domain experts decompose the SUD (functions, data, components, and connections). The resulting model of the SUD include relations between its elements, forming a graph: elements can be refined into sub-elements of the same kind. Functions describe behavior and functionality provided by the SUD and require data, components, and their connections to be executed. Connections link components to each other. Finally, data is stored on components or transmitted using these connections. For example, a hardware component can be decomposed into a CPU, persistent memory and other components. If necessary, components (including their connections) and data can be further refined into lower levels of granularity. Following these strategies, this activity creates a unified representation for the SUD which supports both tracing of changes and systematic identification of security goals and threats. Existing controls in the SUD are documented along with related assets (e.g., the asset "secret key" for the control "AES encryption"). Existing documentation, such as requirement specifications, data flow diagrams, or component diagrams, may serve as input for this activity.

In our healthcare example, the analyst adds the components, data elements, and connections shown in the component diagram in Fig. 2 to the model of the SUD. The new elements encompass the components "PC", "clinic", "database server", and "hard disk drive", along with the relations "component *hard disk drive* is part of component *database server*" and "component *database server* is part of component *clinic*". Likewise, the analyst adds the connection between component "PC" and component "database server" and the data element "patient data" to the model of the SUD. The link between the data element "patient data" and all components and connections which interact with this data element expands the model further. Finally, the analyst maps these new elements to the previously documented function "patient data retrieval". This results in the SUD model depicted in Fig. 3.

The next activity, *Determine Protection Needs*, systematically identifies security goals for the SUD, based on its model. Additionally, potential damages caused by a violation of security goals are estimated using the assessment model. For example, "confidentiality of data *patient data*" in the introduced medical system handling patient data represents a security goal, as a violation results in loss of privacy. Section 4.1 elaborates on our approach in detail.

Once the security goals are identified, we switch from the domain expert's to the security expert's perspective to identify potential threats to the SUD's security goals in the activity *Analyze Threats*. Again, a systematic approach is applied: For all security goals, we identify threats based on the model of the SUD and a catalog of possible threats. To identify applicable threats, we consider the security goal's class and its relation to the model of the SUD. Evaluating the likelihood of an attack incorporates the estimation of the required attack potential to execute a threat. This estimation is based on the combination of a

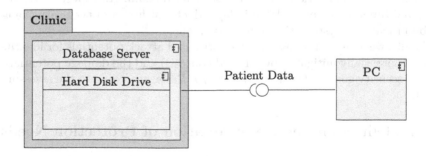

Fig. 2. Exemplary component diagram for the documentation of architectural elements

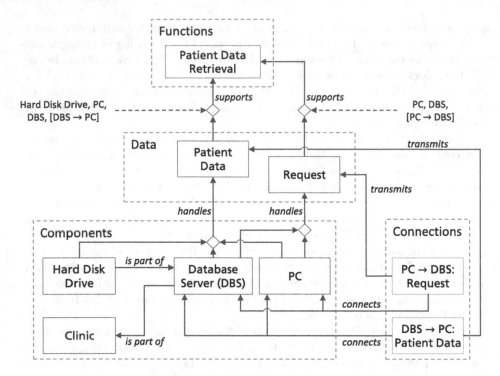

Fig. 3. SUD model for the healthcare example. The "supports" relations from components and connections to the function "Patient Data Retrieval" are summarized by dashed arrows to avoid cluttering of lines in the figure.

set of risk factors such as required expertise, time, knowledge, etc. This approach originates from the Common Methodology for Information Technology Security Evaluation and its application can be simplified through estimates taken from associated predefined threat classes.

Identifying security goals and threats separately yields an important benefit: the model of the SUD and the security goals provide solid ground based on the domain experts' knowledge of the SUD and its environment, while threats are identified based on experience from the security domain. All aspects (i.e., SUD, goals, and threats) can be updated independently at first and necessary changes can be propagated systematically in consequence.

Finally, we assess risks based on the estimated attack potentials for identified threats (potentially mitigated by selected controls) and the damage potentials of affected security goals in the activity *Analyze Risks*, according to the assessment model.

4 Guidelines for the Determination of Protection Needs

In this section, we expand the approach to determine protection needs as described in Sect. 3 by showcasing selected guidelines, which have been applied in multiple risk analysis projects. We present techniques to identify, merge and validate security goals with the aim to document the protection needs of a given SUD as complete, concise, and redundancy-free as possible with respect to the model of the SUD.

4.1 Systematic Identification of Security Goals

To achieve a broad coverage of the protection needs with respect to the model of the SUD, we combine each element of the model (functions, data, components) with each of the *security goal classes* taken from the assessment model (e.g., confidentiality, integrity, availability). This approach results in *potential security goals* such as "confidentiality of data *patient data*", which may also include typically irrelevant results, such as "confidentiality of data *public key*". For each identified potential security goal, we determine damage potentials by assigning damage criteria, i.e., possible damages resulting from a violation of the security goal. E.g., the violation of the confidentiality of a data element may cause "loss of privacy" and "financial damage up to 10.000 $". In this example, "loss of privacy" and "financial damage up to 10.000 $" represent damage criteria, which are defined in the assessment model along with assigned damage potentials, such as "Low", "Moderate", and "High". All potential security goals with non-zero damage potential represent actual security goals, i.e., properties of the SUD that require protection. Thus, we implicitly identify elements of the SUD as *assets* by identifying the security goals (cf. also [5]).

In combination with the security goal classes, the relationships between the elements of the SUD also imply relationships between the security goals. For example, the integrity of a function depends on the integrity of data elements required by the function as well as on the integrity of components processing the function. Thus, MoRA is able to make recommendations for dependencies between security goals and consequently the inheritance of single damage criteria or whole damage potentials for security goals based on their relations to previously estimated security goals. For example, the security goal A: "availability of component *database server*" supports the security goal B: "availability of data *patient data*", as the data "patient data" is stored on the component "database server". Thus, security goal A inherits the damage criteria "delayed medical treatment" and "inappropriate medical treatment" of security goal B.

Additionally, security controls influence the model of the SUD and the security goals and vice versa. On one hand, security controls may introduce new assets into the SUD, such as cryptographic keys for encryption. Consequently, these new assets may lead to the creation of additional security goals, such as "confidentiality of data *secret key*". On the other hand, these security goals in turn influence their related controls, e.g., violation of "confidentiality of data *secret key*" weakens the control "AES encryption". This helps to track the influence of threats on security controls identified in the activity *Analyze Threats*.

Thus, this guideline helps derive the security goals and their relations from known information, namely the SUD, the security goal classes, the damage criteria, security controls, and the MoRA method itself. Consequently, the results are

traceable, comprehensible, and systematically identified. Furthermore, changes
to the SUD can easily be traced and integrated into the risk assessment.

4.2 Merging Security Goals

The approach for a systematic identification of security goals introduced in
Sect. 4.1 strives to produce a complete set of security goals with respect to the
model of the SUD. Therefore, the approach possibly yields a large set of security goals, which may be hard to comprehend for further analysis. Likewise, an
analyst not following this approach may come up with a similarly large set of
security goals, which may additionally contain redundancy. To provide a better
understanding of the protection needs and to avoid redundancy, it is possible
to reduce the number of identified security goals by merging them into more
comprehensible security goals. This guideline introduces a gradual procedure to
aggregate security goals with respect to their attributes, namely the security
goal classes, the referenced architectural or contextual element of the SUD, and
the estimated damage criteria.

First, the method merges redundant security goals: if the security goal class
and the referenced SUD-Element match for two security goals, these can be
merged into a single security goal with all damage criteria of the original security
goals, as showcased in Fig. 4.

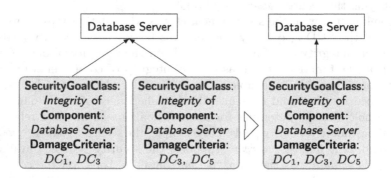

Fig. 4. Merge of redundant security goals (where DC_X represents a damage criterion
from the assessment model)

Iterating on that, the approach for merging security goals can be gradually
expanded. For this step, we use the following relations between elements of the
SUD model as documented in the activity *Document SUD* (cf. Section 3):

– **Refinement:** Elements of the SUD model may refine other elements of the
  same type, e.g., the component "storage device" refines the component "database server".

- **Function mapping:** The SUD model documents which components and data elements are necessary for the implementation of specific functions, creating a relation between those component/data elements and functions. For example, the component "database server" is necessary for the function "patient data retrieval".
- **Data Processing:** The SUD model documents, which data elements are processed (transmitted, received, stored) by components, creating a relation between the component and the data element. For example, the component "database server" stores and transmits the data "patient data".

For two security goals with accordingly related elements of the SUD and an identical set of damage criteria, the method proposes a single merged security goal, containing all of the initial inputs. As this represents a heuristic approach, the analyst has to carefully consider if a merge changes the semantics of the security goals, especially if the security goal classes differ. An example of a merge based on model relations is shown in Fig. 5. The dependency of the security goal "availability of component *database server*" on the security goal "integrity of component *hard disk drive*" hints at a likely valid merge, given that the estimated damage criteria for these security goals are identical, as unavailable and manipulated patient data may both cause delayed or inappropriate medical treatment in this example.

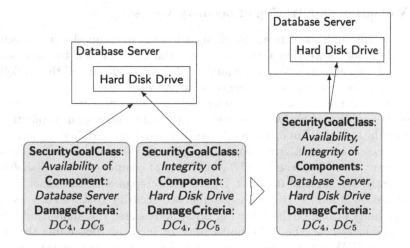

Fig. 5. Merge of security goals with related model elements (refinement).

In an additional step, the method proposes to merge elements with matching security goal classes and identical sets of damage criteria, as showcased in Fig. 6. This aims to improve the comprehensibility of the protection needs by grouping similar security goals. However, the analyst must carefully consider the proposed merges regarding semantic correctness and provide meaningful labels for the

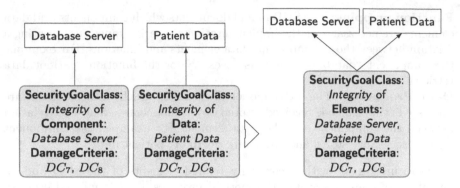

Fig. 6. Merge of security goals with related model elements (data processing).

merged security goals. As in the step described above, the dependencies between security goals indicate likely valid merges.

Finally, the analyst is free to merge any security goals, regardless of security goal class, estimated damage criteria, or type of SUD element. Although the method is able to operate on these security goals, it does not propose any merge except those defined above.

4.3   Validation and Tracing of Security Goals

The aim of this guideline is to enable all stakeholders to comprehend, reproduce, and validate the protection needs based on the SUD model, the assessment model, and the catalogs - even if the analyst did not follow any of the guidelines of MoRA for the creation or merging of security goals.

The method checks for discrepancies between potential security goals and documented security goals (which includes potential security goals explicitly discarded by the analyst). For example, the security goal "availability of component *database server, hard disk drive*" covers the potential security goals "availability of component *database server*" and "availability of component *hard disk drive*". Consequently, the method does not report a discrepancy in this case. An element of the SUD model without a documented security goal for each security goal class hints at one of the following possible reasons: the analyst may have missed a security goal, the SUD model may be incorrect (assuming that each model of the SUD serves a purpose and thus has at least one security goal, an element without any security goals seems unlikely), or the element may serve a structuring purpose, making it only indirectly relevant for the analysis. For example, the component "clinic" houses multiple instances of the component "database server" on an isolated network. Consequently, no security goals for the component "clinic" are documented for the analyzed SUD. However, if the analyst did not document this decision explicitly, the method proposes potential security goals for all security goal classes and the component "clinic".

The modeled relations between SUD elements are utilized to validate the dependencies between security goals. If a relation between SUD elements exists (cf. Section 4.2, Refinement, Function Mapping, Data Processing), then missing dependencies between security goals for these SUD element are reported by the validation. This validation step also considers the respective security goal classes. Vice versa, dependencies between security goals that cannot be deduced from the model of the SUD hint at missing relations in the model or errors regarding the dependencies between security goals and should be checked by the analyst.

The method validates the merged security goals according to the rules defined in Sect. 4.2. Any merged security goals deviating from the rules are highlighted for manual inspection.

The control catalog documents additional assets required for the implementation of controls, such as a trusted root certificate for signature validation. For each introduced control, the method checks whether these required assets are part of the SUD model and whether security goals based on these assets are documented in the protection needs, including their influence on controls. Thus, the method hints at missing assets or security goals.

The method supports change management, tracing, and the comprehensibility of security goals and their attributes. Changes can be traced, as all security goals are mapped to elements of the modeled SUD. Therefore, consequences of changes to the model can be traced to affected security goals. This limits the number of security goals to be examined or adjusted for each change. For example, if the component "database server" in our exemplary healthcare system is replaced with the new component "external cloud service", the security goals for the component "PC" remain unaffected. Likewise, the damage criteria for the security goals of the data element "patient data" remain unchanged. However, the method detects the previously documented dependency of "availability of data *patient data*" on the security goal "availability of component *database server*" as affected by the change, as the latter security goal contains the replaced component "database server". All documented security goals along with their estimated damage criteria are rooted in the application domain. Therefore, domain experts can understand and validate documented security goals. For example, the damage criteria "delayed medical treatment" and "inappropriate medical treatment" are assigned to the security goal "availability of function *retrieve patient data*". As the method also documents dependencies between security goals, more technical security goals, such as "availability of component *hard disk drive*" become more comprehensible, even for people without IT-related background. Finally, as security goals are explicitly related to elements of the SUD, tracing of security goals in later stages of risk assessment (e.g., risk analysis) is supported. For example, the modeled relations between security goals and the model of the SUD can help determine the set of security goals affected by a threat acting on an element of the same model of the SUD.

5   Summary and Conclusion

After a brief summary of our MoRA security risk analysis method, we introduced three practical guidelines for the determination of protection needs. In the first guideline, we showed how to identify security goals systematically, based on MoRA's modeling technique for the system under development and an assessment model tailored to the application domain. In the second guideline, we described how to merge security goals systematically to achieve a more comprehensible and manageable set of security goals as input for later stages of the security risk analysis by applying rules operating on the properties of the documented security goals and model of the SUD. In the third guideline, we presented rules operating on the same properties in order to validate the documented security goals regarding correctness and completeness with respect to the model of the SUD. For all guidelines, we presented examples where we applied the guidelines to a simple fictitious healthcare system.

This method and the presented guidelines have been applied in several industrial development projects. Our experiences show that MoRA's systematic and guided approach induces a good understanding of the subject matter and produces reproducible and comprehensible assessment results. For example, we and a security expert from the application domain independently conducted two security risk analyses of the same SUD. Both analyses produced similar sets of identified risks with similar estimates. However, one identified risk was estimated substantially more critical in our analysis. Owing to our method, we could easily trace and explain the difference: we incorrectly assumed that the analyzed SUD contained business-critical data. Since this was explicitly selected as a damage criterion for one of the affected security goals, it was straightforward to identify this discrepancy and resolve it based on knowledge from the application domain.

A formal description and documentation of the application of our method in appropriate development projects constitutes a task for future work.

References

1. Board, C.C.E.: Common Methodology for Information Technology Security Evaluation – Version 3.1 – Revision 4. Evaluation methodology (2012)
2. BSI. Standard 100-1: Managementsysteme für Informationssicherheit (ISMS). Bonn: Bundesamt für Sicherheit in der Informationstechnik (2008)
3. BSI. Standard 100-2: IT-Grundschutz Vorgehensweise. Bonn: Bundesamt für Sicherheit in der Informationstechnik (2008)
4. BSI. Standard 100-3: Risikoanalyse auf der Basis von IT-Grundschutz. Bonn: Bundesamt für Sicherheit in der Informationstechnik (2008)
5. Eichler, J.: Model-based Security Engineering for Electronic Business Processes. PhD thesis, Technische Universität München (2015)
6. Eichler, J., Angermeier, D.: Modular risk assessment for the development of secure automotive systems. In: 31. VDI/VW-Gemeinschaftstagung Automotive Security (2015)

7. Islam, M.M., Lautenbach, A., Sandberg, C., Olovsson, T.: A risk assessment framework for automotive embedded systems. In: Proceedings of the 2nd ACM International Workshop on Cyber-Physical System Security, pp. 3–14. ACM (2016)
8. ISO/IEC. 15408-1: Information technology – security techniques – evaluation criteria for IT security – part 1: Introduction and general model (2009)
9. ISO/IEC. 31000: Risk management – principles and guidelines (2009)
10. ISO/IEC. 27005: Information technology – security techniques – information security risk management (2011)
11. Kohnfelder, L., Garg, P.: The threats to our products. Microsoft Interface, Microsoft Corporation (1999)
12. Lund, M.S., Solhaug, B., Stølen, K.: Model-Driven Risk Analysis: The CORAS Approach. Springer Science & Business Media, Heidelberg (2010)
13. Mead, N.R., Stehney, T.: Security quality requirements engineering (SQUARE) methodology, vol. 30. ACM (2005)
14. Mellado, D., Fernández-Medina, E., Piattini, M.: A common criteria based security requirements engineering process for the development of secure information systems. Comput. Stan. Interfaces **29**(2), 244–253 (2007)
15. Mouratidis, H., Giorgini, P., Manson, G.: When security meets software engineering: a case of modelling secure information systems. Inf. Syst. **30**(8), 609–629 (2005)
16. O'Connor, M., Das, A.: SQWRL: a query language for OWL. In: Proceedings of the 6th International Conference on OWL: Experiences and Directions, vol. 529, pp. 208–215. CEUR-WS.org (2009)
17. Salini, P., Kanmani, S.: Survey and analysis on security requirements engineering. Comput. Electr. Eng. **38**(6), 1785–1797 (2012)
18. Shostack, A.: Threat Modeling: Designing for Security. Wiley, Hoboken (2014)
19. Souag, A., Salinesi, C., Mazo, R., Comyn-Wattiau, I.: A security ontology for security requirements elicitation. In: Piessens, F., Caballero, J., Bielova, N. (eds.) ESSoS 2015. LNCS, vol. 8978, pp. 157–177. Springer, Cham (2015). doi:10.1007/978-3-319-15618-7_13
20. Tondel, I.A., Jaatun, M.G., Meland, P.H.: Security requirements for the rest of us: a survey. IEEE Softw. **25**(1), 20–27 (2008)
21. Weldemariam, K., Villafiorita, A.: Procedural security analysis: a methodological approach. J. Syst. Softw. **84**(7), 1114–1129 (2011)
22. Wynn, J., Whitmore, J., Upton, G., Spriggs, L., McKinnon, D., McInnes, R., Graubart, R., Clausen, L.: Threat assessment & remediation analysis (TARA): Methodology description version 1.0. Technical report, DTIC Document (2011)

Risk-Based Testing

Design Decisions in the Development of a Graphical Language for Risk-Driven Security Testing

Gencer Erdogan[1(✉)] and Ketil Stølen[1,2]

[1] Department for Software and Service Innovation,
SINTEF Digital, Oslo, Norway
{gencer.erdogan,ketil.stolen}@sintef.no
[2] Department of Informatics, University of Oslo, Oslo, Norway

Abstract. We have developed a domain-specific modeling language named CORAL that employs risk assessment to help security testers select and design test cases based on the available risk picture. In this paper, we present CORAL and then discuss why the language is designed the way it is, and what we could have done differently.

Keywords: Risk-driven security testing · Model-based testing · Security risk assessment · Domain-specific modeling language

1 Introduction

Security testers face the problem of determining tests that are most likely to reveal severe security vulnerabilities. To address this challenge, we have developed a domain-specific modeling language that employs risk assessment to help security testers select and design test cases based on the available risk picture [5]. Our language (CORAL) supports a model-based approach to risk-driven security testing as defined in [2]. The approach is model-based in the sense that graphical models are actively used throughout the whole testing process to support the various testing tasks and activities, and to document the test results.

The intended users of CORAL are security testers. In this paper, we first present CORAL, and then we discuss why the language is designed the way it is, and what we could have done differently. In particular, we motivate our design decisions by discussing five main areas typically considered when developing or evaluating a modeling language: domain appropriateness, comprehensibility appropriateness, participant appropriateness, modeler appropriateness, and tool appropriateness [15]. With respect to what we could have done differently, we discuss alternative design decisions and their consequence in terms of graphical versus textual representations, risk annotations versus tables, choice of modeling notation, CORAL versus attack trees, and CORAL versus formal methods.

The reminder of this paper is organized as follows. In Sect. 2 we present the CORAL language followed by a small example. In Sect. 3 we motivate our

J. Großmann et al. (Eds.): RISK 2016, LNCS 10224, pp. 99–114, 2017.
DOI: 10.1007/978-3-319-57858-3_8

design decisions in context of the five areas mentioned above. In Sect. 4 we discuss alternative design decisions and their consequence. Finally, in Sect. 5 we conclude the paper.

2   The CORAL Language

As shown in Fig. 1, the graphical notation of CORAL is mainly based on the graphical notation of UML sequence diagrams [21]. The graphical icons used to represent risk-related information are based on corresponding graphical icons in the CORAS risk analysis language [17]. With respect to testing concepts, CORAL uses stereotypes from the UML Testing Profile [20]. The constructs in CORAL are grouped into five categories: diagram frame, lifelines, messages, risk-measure annotations, and interaction operators. In the following, we explain each category.

Diagram Frame: The diagram frame is the frame in which a sequence diagram is modeled. A sequence diagram in CORAL may represent the system under test, its environment, as well as threat scenarios that the system under test and its environment are exposed to. The diagram frame is graphically equivalent to the diagram frame in UML used to represent sequence diagrams [21]. Similar to UML, we use the keyword *sd* in a pentagon in the upper left corner of the diagram frame to denote that the diagram is a sequence diagram.

Lifelines: According to UML, a lifeline represents an individual participant in an interaction [21]. As illustrated in Fig. 1, we distinguish between five different lifelines: general lifeline, deliberate threat lifeline, accidental threat lifeline, non-human threat lifeline, and asset lifeline.

The general lifeline is graphically equivalent to a lifeline used in UML sequence diagrams. In CORAL, a general lifeline is used to model the system under test, as well as the environment interacting with the system under test. The name of the lifeline is placed inside the rectangle of the lifeline as illustrated in Fig. 1, and the naming convention is equivalent to the naming convention of lifelines in UML.

The lifelines representing threats are used to model threats that may initiate threat scenarios, which in turn may cause security risks in the system under test. Inspired by CORAS [17], we distinguish between three kinds of threats: deliberate threat, accidental threat, and non-human threat. A deliberate threat is a human threat that has malicious intents. An accidental threat is also a human threat, but this threat is different in the sense that it does not have malicious intents. The non-human threat is a threat that may be anything else except a human. For example, a power failure in a server hall may cause problems with respect to the availability of a system.

In practice, the distinction between a human threat and a non-human threat is sometimes not straight forward. For example, if a hacker exploits a security bug in a source code in order to attack a system, then the threat is the hacker. On the other hand, if the security bug lies dormant in the source code and is

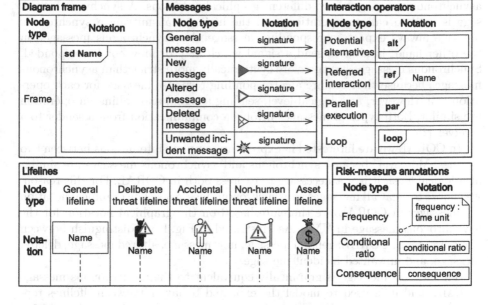

Fig. 1. CORAL graphical notation.

triggered at some point during system execution, then the threat is the bug in the source code, that is, a non-human threat. In other words, the distinction between a human threat and a nonhuman threat depends on the viewpoint from which a threat is regarded. The name of a threat is placed below the icon representing the threat as illustrated in Fig. 1.

The name of a threat typically represents a threat profile which is described by the tester. A threat may be named, for example, "hacker" (deliberate threat), "database administrator" (accidental threat), or "computer virus" (non-human threat).

In CORAL, risk assessment is carried out with respect to security assets we want to protect. Security assets are represented by the asset lifeline shaped as a moneybag, and the asset name is placed below the moneybag icon. Examples of security assets are "availability of customer data" or "integrity of bank transactions". What is meant by "customer data" and "bank transactions" has to be described by the tester.

Messages: According to UML, a message defines a particular communication between lifelines of an interaction [21]. UML distinguish between complete, lost and found messages. Complete messages have both a sender and a receiver lifeline. A lost message has a sender lifeline, but not a receiver lifeline. A found message has a receiver lifeline, but not a sender lifeline. The graphical notation for these messages are different. However, lost and found messages are often unnecessary and are used in rare situations [25]. Furthermore, UML categorize complete messages into synchronous and asynchronous messages. The synchronous and asynchronous messages have different graphical notations. A synchronous message is used to call an operation, and the lifeline transmitting a synchronous message always expects a responding message. An asynchronous message, on the other hand, is used to send a signal which may or may not be responded. Synchronous messages are therefore syntactically more strict than asynchronous messages because they require a corresponding response message for each operation call. However, at a logical level, sending a signal and calling an operation are similar. Both types of messages involve a communication from a sender to a receiver [25].

In CORAL we are interested in expressing complete interactions between two lifelines. Moreover, because synchronous and asynchronous messages are similar at a logical level, it is not necessary to express both in CORAL. For this reason, we choose to treat all messages as asynchronous messages. The graphical notation for messages in CORAL are therefore based on the graphical notation for the asynchronous message in UML. As illustrated in Fig. 1, we distinguish between five messages in CORAL: general message, new message, altered message, deleted message, and unwanted incident message.

The general message is graphically equivalent to the asynchronous message in UML, and it is used to model the expected behavior between lifelines representing the system under test and its environment, that is, the interaction between general lifelines (recall that general lifelines are used to model the system under test and its environment). The signature of a message, that is, the content of a message, is placed above the arrow representing the message. Signatures are written using the same convention as given for messages in UML. In addition, we represent the risk related information, in the signatures, using a red-colored, bold, and italic font to distinguish between the expected behavior and the risk-related information.

New, altered, deleted and unwanted incident messages are used in combination to represent threat scenarios. A new message is a message initiated by a threat. This may be a deliberate human threat, an accidental human threat, or a non-human threat. A new message is represented by a red triangle which is placed at the transmitting end of the message. An altered message is a message in the system under test that has been altered by a threat to deviate from its expected behavior. Altered messages are represented by a triangle with red borders and white fill. A deleted message is a message in the system under test that has been deleted by a threat. Deleted messages are represented by a triangle with red borders and a red cross in the middle of the triangle. Finally, an unwanted incident message is a message modeling that an asset is harmed or its value is reduced. Unwanted incidents are represented by a yellow explosion sign.

Risk-Measure Annotations: Risk-measure annotations are used to annotate messages for the purpose of estimating and evaluating security risks. As illustrated in Fig. 1, we distinguish between three kinds of risk-measure annotations: frequency, conditional ratio, and consequence.

The frequency annotation represents either the frequency of the transmission or the frequency of the reception of a message. The graphical notation of a frequency annotation is equivalent to the graphical notation of a comment generally used in UML [21]. The connector on the frequency annotation is attached on either the transmission-end or the reception-end of a general, new, or altered message. It may also be attached on the transmission-end of an unwanted incident message to convey how often an unwanted incident harms a certain security asset. A frequency annotation may not be attached on a deleted message because the message represents a complete deletion. That is, if a message is deleted, then it is not transmitted and therefore not received. It therefore does not make sense to estimate how often a message is *not* received, given that it is *not* transmitted. A message is either deleted, or it is not. Also, in the context of testing, we are interested in testing the messages that may *cause* the deletion of other messages. The frequency is written inside the comment frame, in terms of an interval followed by a time unit, as illustrated in Fig. 1.

The conditional ratio annotation represents the ratio by which a message is received, given that it is transmitted. Conditional ratios may be attached on general, new, or altered messages, and may not be attached on deleted messages because they represent complete deletion. In addition, conditional ratios may not be attached on unwanted incidents because their purpose is to model that an asset is harmed or reduced in value.

The consequence annotation represents the impact an unwanted incident has on an asset. Thus, consequences may therefore be attached only on unwanted incident messages.

Interaction Operators: In sequence diagrams, messages may be combined in rectangles containing special keywords in order to convey a particular relationship between the combined messages. The rectangle encapsulating the messages is referred to as a combined fragment, while the keyword is referred to as an interaction operator. An interaction operator specifies the operation that defines the semantics of the combination of messages [21]. As illustrated in Fig. 1, CORAL makes use of four interaction operators inherited from UML: potential alternatives (keyword *alt*), referred interaction (keyword *ref*), parallel execution (keyword *par*), and loop (keyword *loop*). All interactions in sequence diagrams are by default encapsulated within an implicit combined fragment that makes use of an interaction operator named weak sequencing (keyword *seq*). The *seq* operator is the implicit composition mechanism of interactions. However, because the *seq* operator is always implicitly included in all sequence diagrams, it is generally not modeled explicitly. The reader is referred to UML for further information on interaction operators [21].

2.1 Example-Driven Explanation of the CORAL Approach

We carry out risk-driven security testing in three consecutive phases: test planning, security risk assessment, and security testing. The method takes as input a description of the system to test, and provides a test report as output. The description may be in the form of system diagrams and models, use case documentation, source code, executable versions of the system, and so on.

In Phase 1 we prepare the system model, identify security assets to be protected, define frequency and consequence scales, and define the risk evaluation matrix based on the frequency and consequence scales.

In Phase 2 we carry out risk modeling in three consecutive steps. First, we identify security risks by analyzing the system model with respect to the security assets, and then we identify threat scenarios that may cause the security risks. Second, we estimate frequency and consequence of the identified risks by making use of the predefined frequency and consequence scales, respectively. Third, we evaluate the risks with respect to their frequency and consequence estimates and select the most severe risks to test.

In Phase 3 we conduct security testing in three consecutive steps. First, for each risk selected for testing we select its associated threat scenario and specify a test objective for that threat scenario. To obtain a test case fulfilling the test objective, we annotate the threat scenario with stereotypes from the UML Testing Profile [20] according to the test objective. Second, we carry out security testing with respect to the test cases. Finally, based on the test results, we write a test report.

The example in Fig. 2 is a small fragment taken from an industrial case study, which is thoroughly documented in [4]. The system under test is a feature in a web-based e-business application designed to deliver streamlined administration and reporting of all forms of equity-based compensation plans. The feature is named Exercise Options and it is used for buying shares in a company.

Phase 1 (test planning): We modeled Exercise Options from a black-box perspective by observing its behavior. That is, we executed Exercise Options using a web browser, observed its behavior, and created the model based on that (Fig. 2a). Together with the system owners we decided to focus on security risks that may be introduced via the application layer. Thus, the threat profile is someone who has access to Exercise Options, but who resides outside the network boundaries of the service provider. We identified security assets by consulting the system owners. The security asset identified for Exercise Options was *integrity of data*.

We also defined a frequency scale and a consequence scale together with the system owner. The frequency scale consisted of five values (Certain, Likely, Possible, Unlikely, and Rare), where each value was defined as a frequency interval. For example, the frequency interval for likelihood Possible was $[5,20\rangle{:}1y$, which means "from and including 5 to less than 20 times per year". The consequence scale also consisted of five values (Catastrophic, Major, Moderate, Minor, and Insignificant), where each value described the impact by which the security asset is harmed. For example, consequence Major with respect to security asset *integrity of data* was defined as "the integrity of customer shares is compromised". The scales were also used to construct a 5×5 risk evaluation matrix used to evaluate risks in Phase 2.

Phase 2 (security risk assessment): We identified security risks by analyzing the model in Fig. 2a with respect to security asset *integrity of data*. We did this by first identifying unwanted incidents. Then we identified alterations that have

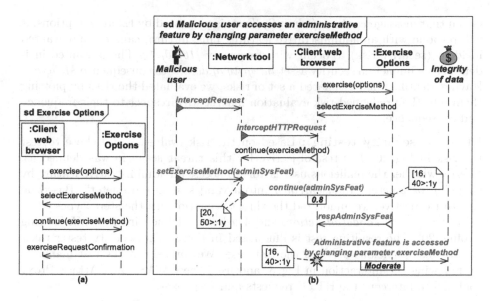

Fig. 2. (a) Black-box model of Exercise Options. (b) Threat scenario.

to take place in the messages in order to cause the unwanted incidents. Finally we identified messages initiated by the threat which in turn could cause the alterations.

Let us consider a threat scenario for the black-box model of Exercise Options. Assume that a malicious user attempts to access an administrative feature by altering certain parameters in the HTTP request sent to Exercise Options. The malicious user could achieve this, for example, by first intercepting the request containing the message *continue(exerciseMethod)* using a network proxy tool such as OWASP ZAP [22], and then altering the parameter *exerciseMethod* in the message as an attempt to access other features in the system. This alteration, could in turn give the malicious user access to an administrative feature. This unwanted incident occurs if the alteration is successfully carried out, and Exercise Options responds with an administrative feature instead of the expected message *exerciseRequestConfirmation*. Thus, the unwanted incident may occur after the reception of message *exerciseRequestConfirmation* (Fig. 2a). The resulting threat scenario is shown in Fig. 2b.

In order to estimate how often threat scenarios may occur, in terms of frequency, we based ourselves on knowledge data bases such as OWASP [22], reports and papers published within the software security community, as well as expert knowledge within security testing. We see from Fig. 2b that the malicious user successfully alters the parameter *exerciseMethod* with frequency *[20,50⟩:1y*. Given that parameter *exerciseMethod* is successfully altered and transmitted, it will be received by Exercise Options with conditional ratio *0.8*. The conditional ratio causes the new frequency *[16,40⟩:1y* for the reception of message *continue(adminSysFeat)*. This is calculated by multiplying *[20,50⟩:1y* with *0.8*.

Given that message *continue(adminSysFeat)* is processed by Exercise Options, it will respond with an administrative feature. This, in turn, causes the unwanted incident (security risk) to occur with frequency *[16,40⟩:1y*. The unwanted incident has an impact on security asset *integrity of data* with consequence *Moderate*. Having identified and estimated a set of risks, we evaluated the risks by plotting them into the predefined risk evaluation matrix with respect to their frequency and consequence.

Phase 3 (security testing): Based on the risk evaluation we chose to test the risk in Fig. 2b. The test objective for this threat scenario was defined as: "Verify whether the malicious user is able to access an administrative feature by changing parameter *exerciseMethod* into a valid system parameter". Based on this test objective, we annotated the threat scenario with the stereotypes *SUT*, *TestComponent*, *ValidationAction*, and *Verdict* as defined in the UML Testing Profile [20]. The resulting test is illustrated in Fig. 3. The security tester takes the role as "malicious user" in the test case. We carried out the test manually by following the interaction in Fig. 3, and used the OWASP Zed Attack Proxy tool [22] to intercept the HTTP requests and responses.

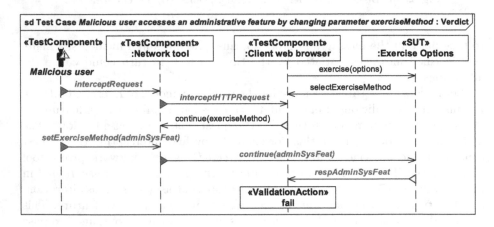

Fig. 3. Security test w.r.t. the threat scenario in Fig. 2b.

3   Why We Designed CORAL as We Did?

There are five main areas to consider when developing or evaluating a modeling language: domain appropriateness, comprehensibility appropriateness, participant appropriateness, modeler appropriateness, and tool appropriateness [15]. Organizational appropriateness may also be considered [15], but this is outside the scope of this paper because CORAL is not developed for a specific organization. Thus, in the following, we elaborate on why we designed CORAL as we did with respect to the first five aforementioned areas.

3.1 Domain Appropriateness

Domain appropriateness relates the modeling language to the domain it targets [15]. The purpose is to evaluate expressiveness of the language in relation to the domain. This also includes considering whether the language miss any constructs (construct incompleteness), and whether the language expresses anything that is not in the domain (construct excess).

CORAL employs constructs that are well known within the domain of testing, security, and risk assessment. The conceptual foundation of CORAL is leading international standards. Concepts related to testing are based on the software testing standard ISO 29119 [12] and the UML Testing Profile [20]. Concepts related to security are based on the information security standard ISO 27000 [10]. Concepts related to security risk assessment are based on the information security risk management standard ISO 27005 [11]. Moreover, the graphical notation of CORAL is based on UML sequence diagrams, which are among the top three modeling languages within the model-based testing community [19], and often used for testing purposes [27]. In addition, constructs inherited from UML sequence diagrams are annotated with risk-related information such as threat, unwanted incident, and security asset, which in turn brings security risk assessment to the work bench of testers without the burden of a separate risk analysis language. The CORAL process of risk assessment involves security risk modeling. The resulting risk models are used as a basis for designing and subsequently executing security tests.

The above standards and guidelines consist of a large number of concepts relevant for their respective domains. When developing CORAL we selected and related concepts which we found necessary for security testers to carry out risk-driven security testing. Security testers may carry out a complete run of risk-driven security testing using constructs provided in CORAL. This is backed up by an empirical evaluation in which we discovered that CORAL is effective in terms of producing valid risk models and identifying security tests [4].

3.2 Comprehensibility Appropriateness

Comprehensibility appropriateness relates the language to the social actor interpretation [15]. This is often evaluated with respect to design principles referred to as semiotic clarity, perceptual discriminability, complexity management, cognitive integration, visual expressiveness, dual coding, and graphic economy [18].

Each graphical symbol in CORAL is designed to represents only one semantic construct in the language. For example, the graphical icon shaped as a human with "devil horns" represents a deliberate threat, and may not be used to represent accidental threats or non-human threats, and so on. Moreover, each semantic construct in CORAL is represented by only one graphical symbol. For example, an unwanted incident is only represented by the unwanted incident message, and may not be represented by other messages. This means that CORAL fulfills the principle of semiotic clarity [18].

The principle of perceptual discriminability states that different symbols should be clearly distinguishable from each other. To achieve this we employ distinct shapes and colors. Although the conditional ratio symbol and the consequence symbol are rectangular, they are easily distinguishable because conditional ratios may be assigned to general, new, and altered messages, while consequences are assigned only to unwanted incident messages. In addition, conditional ratios are always represented as nonnegative real numbers, while consequences are always represented textually. However, the new, altered, and deleted messages are similar in the sense that they all have a triangular shape at the transmission end, but they are distinguishable with respect to the coloring inside the triangles. In our experience, CORAL risk models typically contain a greater number of new messages compared to the number of altered and deleted messages. In some cases, particularly in large risk models, this makes it somewhat difficult to spot the altered/deleted messages. We may mitigate this by using different shapes at the transmission end on new, altered and deleted messages. However, the reason why we use triangles (in combination with the color red) is to support semantic transparency, which is discussed in Sect. 3.3.

With respect to the principle of complexity management, our experience shows that the *ref* construct is sufficient to manage the complexity of CORAL risk models [3–5]. Because of its modular property, the *ref* construct may also be used to support cognitive integration, i.e., to support integration of information from different diagrams. Although the information in a *ref* construct is limited to abstract descriptions of the referred interaction, it is sufficient for constructing high-level risk models, which are useful to obtain an overview of the various threat scenarios and their relationships. Thus, in CORAL we may divide complex risk models into simpler risk models, as well as compose high-level risk models, by making use of the *ref* construct.

The principles of visual expressiveness and dual coding refer to the usage of the full range and capacities of visual variables, and the usage of text to complement graphics, respectively. To achieve this we use a red colored, bold, and italic font to highlight the risk-related information (text) on messages. This comes in addition to symbols that are distinguishable with respect to shape and color. Based on our experience, this convention is useful for new and altered messages, as well as unwanted incidents. The text on new messages is always formatted as risk-related information because these messages are initiated by threats. The text on altered messages is formatted as risk-related information when highlighting the alteration in the message. This could be part of the text or the complete text on the altered message. The text on unwanted incidents are always formatted as risk-related information because they represent that assets are harmed or reduced in value. This formatting strengthens the visual expressiveness and helps security testers keep track of and distinguish between risk-related and non risk-related information on the messages.

The principle of graphic economy states that the number of different graphical symbols should not exceed 6 in order to be cognitively manageable. However, if a language consists of more than 6 symbols, which is the case in CORAL, then one can deal with graphic complexity by increasing visual expressiveness. As explained above, to achieve this we format text to complement the graphics, which in turn strengthens the visual expressiveness. In particular, we position the symbols representing new, altered, deleted, and unwanted incident messages so that they are horizontally aligned with the message, as well as correctly oriented with respect to the message direction. These two visual variables give an additional increase to the visual expressiveness [18].

3.3 Participant Appropriateness

Participant appropriateness relates the participant knowledge to the language [15]. This is often evaluated with respect to the design principle referred to as semantic transparency [18].

The principle of semantic transparency states that symbols should use visual representations whose appearance suggests their meaning. To achieve this, we base the risk-related symbols used in CORAL on corresponding symbols used in the CORAS risk analysis language [17]. The graphical symbols in CORAS have been empirically shown to be cognitively effective [8], and these concepts are also commonly used in security testing [23], which is why we use similar symbols in CORAL.

3.4 Modeler Appropriateness

Modeler appropriateness relates the language to the knowledge of the one doing the modeling [15]. This is often evaluated with respect to the design principle referred to as cognitive fit [18].

The principle of cognitive fit states that the language should use different visual dialects for different tasks and audiences. CORAL is mainly to be used by security testers, for the purpose of risk-driven security testing. This implies that CORAL must provide concepts and a corresponding graphical notation necessary to carry out security risk assessment, as well as security testing. As discussed above, we provide this by basing CORAL on state of the art standards and guidelines. However, this also means that CORAL requires testers to be familiar with security risk assessment. Security testers usually have this required background, because they often have to carry out activities related to security risk assessment, such as creating security abuse/misuse cases, performing architectural risk analysis, and building risk-driven security test plans [23].

3.5 Tool Appropriateness

Tool appropriateness relates the language to the interpretation from the technical audience (tools) [15]. A prerequisite for tool interpretation is that the language must have a syntax and semantics that are formally defined. CORAL is accompanied by an abstract syntax as well as a schematically defined natural-language semantics [3]. Testers may use the abstract syntax in order to create risk models that are syntactically correct, and the natural-language semantics in order to clearly and consistently document, communicate and analyze risks.

4   What We Could Have Done Differently?

This section discusses what we could have done differently with respect to the design of CORAL.

4.1   Graphical Versus Textual

A model may be either two-dimensional or one-dimensional[1]. A graph is two-dimensional while text is one-dimensional. CORAL is obviously two-dimensional. A one-dimensional alternative would be to replace the UML diagrams by actual code and the specific graphical annotations of CORAL by textual annotations. One argument in favor of such an approach is that it would be sufficient for the tester to know the source-code language. However, the price to pay would be no abstraction. The tester would have to create a mental model of how security risks are caused including the chain of events and how they may affect the system to test, and based on that describe the risk picture. Moreover, the tester would have to read through code from top to bottom to capture details such as unwanted incidents, frequencies, conditional probabilities, consequences and so on.

Using UML sequence diagrams we cover a scenario that occurs multiple times in the source code by a single diagram. Moreover, UML sequence diagrams capture the interaction between independent actors and processes in a manner not possible using source code. Finally, UML sequence diagrams allow us to describe the behavior of human actors including working procedures as well as threat behavior.

Finding the right balance between text and graphics in annotations is nontrivial. As argued in [6], text labels are often preferred over graphical means. Hence, finding the right balance is essential. The recently completed EMFASE project arrived at similar conclusions [1].

4.2   Risk Annotations Versus Tables

An alternative to the CORAL approach of representing risk-related information on top of sequence diagrams is to document the risk-related information separately using tables. The most commonly used table-based risk assessment approach is Hazard and Operability (HazOp) analysis [9]. Many risk-driven testing approaches use table-representations inspired from HazOp analysis [2]. HazOp makes use of guide words to identify risks, their causes, as well as possible treatments. Figure 4 illustrates a typical HazOp table in which we represent the threat scenario in Fig. 2b.

Tables may also be regarded as two-dimensional because a cell in the table can be identified by pairs of row and column headings. Moreover, tables present all information consistently with respect to the headings. This guides the reader to the relevant information in a structured manner. Finally, information in tables

---

[1] A model may of course also be three-dimensional, but that is not relevant in this paper.

Element	Characteristics	Guide word	Deviation	Possible causes	Consequences	Safeguards	Comments	Action required
Exercise Options form	Selling or buying shares in a company	No (not)	HTTP requests not sanitized	Web-application form has no input validation	An admin-feature is accessed	No	HTTP requests may have been tampered to access restricted features	Implement input validation mechanizm

Fig. 4. HazOp table representing the threat scenario in Fig. 2b.

are generally presented as text. This removes the need to interpret semantics of graphical symbols when looking for certain information.

CORAL is based on the hypothesis that it is advantageous to annotate risk information on the locations where it belongs in a style corresponding to the underlying modeling language. For example, the transmission frequency of message *continue(adminSysFeat)* in Fig. 2b is attached to the transmission-end of the message, while the reception frequency is attached to the reception-end. Moreover, a particular location in the diagram may convey more than one kind of information. For example, the transmission-end of message *continue(adminSysFeat)* in Fig. 2b simultaneously conveys that the message is a *new message*, that the transmission occurs with frequency *[20, 50⟩:1y*, and that it is transmitted by *Network tool*. This information would normally be found in separate columns in a table.

On the other hand, whether tables are better than graphs or the other way around is far from obvious [16]. The answer depends probably on the context of use and the complexity of the information to be presented.

4.3 Sequence Diagrams Versus Other UML Representations

The graphical notation of CORAL could have been based on modeling languages other than UML sequence diagrams. According to Dias-Neto et al. [19], the three most common modeling notations (not including UML sequence diagrams) used in model-based testing are UML state machines/finite state machines, class diagrams, and use-case diagrams.

State machines are specifications of sequences of states that an object or an interaction goes through in response to events during its life, together with its responsive effects [21]. These sequence of states correspond to events that occur chronologically on a particular lifeline in CORAL. In principle, it is possible to represent the same risk-related information as in CORAL using state machines. The advantage of sequence diagrams when compared to state machines is that we may easily isolate particular scenarios without having to consider the behavior for other scenarios. This is very much in the spirit of testing and an important reason for the development of sequence diagram notation.

Class diagrams capture the static view of a system as a collection of declarative (static) model elements with contents and relationships [21]. To this end, class diagrams are useful to describe the structure of the system to test.

However, the kind of dynamic behavior that CORAL address cannot be specified using class diagrams.

Use-case diagrams show the relationships among actors and use cases within a system [21]. Their high-level nature is useful for capturing high-level threat scenarios a system may be exposed to. A threat can be modeled as an actor, while a high-level scenario corresponds to use-case. Misuse cases [26] is a well-known notation based on use-case diagrams used to capture high-level threat scenarios. However, in the context of testing, high-level threat scenarios are only useful as a starting point to design detailed security tests. CORAL addresses the latter, that is, designing detailed security tests.

4.4   CORAL Versus Attack Trees

The annotation of sequence diagrams may be thought of as augmenting the sequence diagrams with an attack tree on which there is a huge literature [14]. CORAL allows the representation of sequential conjunction [13] and disjunction, but not ordinary conjunction, for which we have not seen any real need. Instead of embedding the CORAL annotations within the sequence diagrams we could of course used attack trees in addition to sequence diagrams in the same way as some approaches to risk-driven testing use tables in addition to the system documentation. However, as for tables, we think intended users benefit from an integrated approach.

4.5   CORAL Versus Formal Methods

CORAL is supported by an abstract textual syntax formalized in EBNF [3]. The semantics of CORAL is defined by a schematic translation of any syntactically correct CORAL expression into English sentences. The target audience of the natural-language semantics is security testers, and the purpose is to help testers clearly and consistently document, communicate and analyze security risks.

Although formal in the sense described above, CORAL is not formal in the classical meaning of formal methods. This would require a mathematical semantics as well as a formalization of the natural-language expressions used to annotate CORAL diagrams. A mathematical semantics would indeed be useful, not to replace the natural-language semantics which targets the users of CORAL, but to allow tool and method developers building on CORAL prove soundness of the rules and heuristics.

Formalizing the natural-language expressions would on the other hand be counter-productive. We believe it is a strength of CORAL that security testers freely can augment their diagrams without being constrained by formal concerns.

To summarize, a formal semantics would be beneficial and we hope to provide this in the future, for example, based on STAIRS [7] or probabilistic STAIRS [24] for sequence diagrams. Formalizing the natural-language expressions would probably alienate the CORAL approach from its intended users, namely security testers.

5   Conclusion

In this paper we have presented the CORAL language for risk-driven security testing, motivated some of the major design decisions on which it builds, and discussed what we could have done differently with respect to the design of the language.

The target audience of CORAL is security testers. We have tried to explain why we think CORAL is comprehensible to security testers and why it is appropriate to use for risk-driven security testing.

With respect to what we could have done differently we considered various alternatives and their impact on CORAL. In particular, we discussed why we decided to develop CORAL as a graphical language instead of augmenting code, why we embed risk-related annotations in sequence diagrams instead of using separate tables or attack trees, why we do not build on other UML notations instead of sequence diagrams, and why formalizing the natural-language expressions in CORAL diagrams is counter-productive.

Acknowledgments. This work has been conducted as part of the EMFASE project funded by SESAR Joint Undertaking (SESAR WP-E project, 2013–2016) managed by Eurocontrol, and the AGRA project (236657) funded by the Research Council of Norway under the BIA research programme.

References

1. Empirical Framework for Security Design and Economic Trade-Off (EMFASE) (2016). https://securitylab.disi.unitn.it/doku.php?id=emfase. Accessed 21 Apr 2016
2. Erdogan, G., Li, Y., Runde, R.K., Seehusen, F., Stølen, K.: Approaches for the combined use of risk analysis and testing: a systematic literature review. Int. J. Softw. Tools Technol. Transfer **16**(5), 627–642 (2014)
3. Erdogan, G., Refsdal, A., Stølen, K.: Schematic Generation of English-prose Semantics for a Risk Analysis Language Based on UML Interactions. Technical report A26407, SINTEF Information and Communication Technology (2014)
4. Erdogan, G., Stølen, K., Aagedal, J.Ø.: Evaluation of the CORAL approach for risk-driven security testing based on an industrial case study. In: Proceedings of the 2nd International Conference on Information Systems Security and Privacy (ICISSP 2016), pp. 219–226. SCITEPRESS (2016)
5. Erdogan, G.: CORAL: A Model-Based Approach to Risk-Driven Security Testing. Ph.D. thesis, University of Oslo (2015)
6. Grøndahl, I.H., Lund, M.S., Stølen, K.: Reducing the effort to comprehend risk models: text labels are often preferred over graphical means. Risk Anal. **31**(11), 1813–1831 (2011)
7. Haugen, Ø., Husa, K.E., Runde, R.K., Stølen, K.: STAIRS towards formal design with sequence diagrams. Softw. Syst. Model. **4**(4), 355–357 (2005)
8. Hogganvik, I., Stølen, K.: A graphical approach to risk identification, motivated by empirical investigations. In: Nierstrasz, O., Whittle, J., Harel, D., Reggio, G. (eds.) MODELS 2006. LNCS, vol. 4199, pp. 574–588. Springer, Heidelberg (2006). doi:10.1007/11880240_40

9. International Electrotechnical Commission. IEC 61882, Hazard and Operability studies (HAZOP studies) - Application guide (2001)

10. International Organization for Standardization. ISO/IEC 27000: 2009(E), Information technology - Security techniques - Information security management systems - Overview and vocabulary (2009)

11. International Organization for Standardization. ISO/IEC 27005: 2011(E), Information technology - Security techniques - Information security risk management (2011)

12. International Organization for Standardization. ISO/IEC/IEEE 29119–1: 2013(E), Software and system engineering - Software testing - Part 1: Concepts and definitions (2013)

13. Jhawar, R., Kordy, B., Mauw, S., Radomirović, S., Trujillo-Rasua, R.: Attack trees with sequential conjunction. In: Federrath, H., Gollmann, D. (eds.) SEC 2015. IAICT, vol. 455, pp. 339–353. Springer, Cham (2015). doi:10.1007/978-3-319-18467-8_23

14. Kordy, B., Piètre-Cambacédès, L., Schweitzer, P.: DAG-based attack and defense modeling: Dont miss the forest for the attack trees. Comput. Sci. Rev. **13–14**, 1–38 (2014)

15. Krogstie, J.: Model-Based Development and Evolution of Information Systems - A Quality Approach. Springer, London (2012)

16. Labunets, K., Li, Y., Massacci, F., Paci, F., Ragosta, M., Solhaug, B., Stølen, K., Tedeschi, A.: Preliminary Experiments on the Relative Comprehensibility of Tabular and Graphical Risk Models. In: Fifth SESAR Innovation Days, pp. 1–7. SESAR WPE (2015)

17. Lund, M.S., Solhaug, B., Stølen, K.: Analysis, Model-Driven Risk: The CORAS Approach. Springer, Heidelberg (2011)

18. Moody, D.L.: The "physics" of notations: toward a scientific basis for constructing visual notations in software engineering. IEEE Trans. Software Eng. **35**(6), 756–779 (2009)

19. Dias Neto, A.C., Subramanyan, R., Vieira, M., Travassos, G.H.: A survey on model-based testing approaches: a systematic review. In: Proceedings of the 1st ACM International Workshop on Empirical Assessment of Software Engineering Languages and Technologies (WEASELTech 2007), pp. 31–36. ACM (2007)

20. Object Management Group. UML Testing Profile (UTP), version 1.2: formal/2013-04-03

21. Object Management Group. Unified Modeling Language (UML), version 2.5: formal/2015-03-01

22. Open Web Application Security Project (2016). https://www.owasp.org/index.php/Main_Page. Accessed 20 Apr 2016

23. Potter, B., McGraw, G.: Software security testing. IEEE Secur. Priv. **2**(5), 81–85 (2004)

24. Refsdal, A., Runde, R.K., Stølen, K.: Stepwise refinement of sequence diagrams with soft real-time constraints. J. Comput. Syst. Sci. **81**(7), 1221–1251 (2015)

25. Rumbaugh, J., Jacobson, I., Booch, G.: The Unified Modeling Language Reference Manual, 2nd edn. Addison-Wesley, Boston (2005)

26. Sindre, G., Opdahl, A.L.: Eliciting security requirements with misuse cases. Requirements Eng. **10**(1), 34–44 (2005)

27. Utting, M., Pretschner, A., Legeard, B.: A taxonomy of model-based testing approaches. Softw. Test. Verification Reliab. **22**(5), 297–312 (2012)

A Lightweight Approach for Estimating Probability in Risk-Based Software Testing

Rudolf Ramler[1]([✉]), Michael Felderer[2], and Matthias Leitner[2]

[1] Software Competence Center Hagenberg GmbH,
Softwarepark 21, 4232 Hagenberg, Austria
rudolf.ramler@scch.at

[2] Department of Computer Science, University of Innsbruck,
Technikerstrasse 21a, 6020 Innsbruck, Austria
{michael.felderer,matthias.leitner}@uibk.ac.at

Abstract. Using risk information in testing is requested in many testing strategies and recommended by international standards. The resulting, widespread awareness creates an increasing demand for concrete implementation guidelines and for methodological support on risk-based testing. In practice, however, many companies still perform risk-based testing in an informal way, based only on expert opinion or intuition. In this paper we address the task of quantifying risks by proposing a lightweight approach for estimating risk probabilities. The approach follows the "yesterday's weather" principle used for planning in Extreme Programming. Probability estimates are based on the number of defects in the previous version. This simple heuristic can easily be implemented as part of risk-based testing without specific prerequisites. It suits the need of small and medium enterprises as well as agile environments which have neither time nor resources for establishing elaborated approaches and procedures for data collection and analysis. To investigate the feasibility of the approach we used historical defect data from a popular open-source application. Our estimates for three consecutive versions achieved an accuracy of 73% to 78% and showed a low number of critical overestimates (<4%) and few underestimates (<1%). For practical risk-based testing such estimates provide a reliable quantitative basis that can be easily augmented with the expert knowledge of human decision-makers. Furthermore, these results also define a baseline for future research on improving probability estimation approaches.

Keywords: Risk-based testing · Risk assessment · Probability estimation · Defect prediction · Test management · Software testing

1 Introduction

Risk-based testing is a testing approach which considers risks related to a software product as the guiding factor to support decisions in all phases of the test process [1]. As the recently published international standard for software testing, ISO/IEC/IEEE 29119 [2] explicitly involves risks as an integral part of the testing process, there is increasing demand for methodological support on risk-based testing.

© Springer International Publishing AG 2017
J. Großmann et al. (Eds.): RISK 2016, LNCS 10224, pp. 115–128, 2017.
DOI: 10.1007/978-3-319-57858-3_9

In general, a *risk* is an event that may possibly occur and, if it occurs, it has negative consequences. Risks are determined by the two factors *probability* and *impact*. The factor probability describes the likelihood that the negative event, e.g. a software failure, occurs and impact characterizes the cost if the failure occurs in operation. Assessing the risk exposure of a software feature or component requires estimating both factors. Impact can usually be derived from the business value associated to the feature defined in the software requirements specification. Probability is influenced by the implementation characteristics of the feature or component as well as the usage context in which the software system is applied.

Identifying and estimating risks is a core activity in risk-based testing. Nevertheless, we observed that many companies do not follow established approaches. In a study on risk-based testing we investigated the daily practice of software testing in several large and small companies [3, 4]. Especially small and medium enterprises do not systematically estimate risks and, if they do, they mostly rely on expert opinion. While expert opinion is a valuable source for risk information, experts seem to underestimate the probability of risks and may produce contradicting as well as misleading estimates [5].

In this paper we present a lightweight approach to estimating the risk probability in risk-based software testing and its evaluation. The application context mainly considered in this paper is functional testing, although the approach may as well be applied for testing a wide spectrum of functional and non-functional properties of a software system. The emphasis of the approach is on being lightweight, i.e., simple in its design and simple in its application. The aim of this paper is to explore "the simplest thing that could possibly work" [6]. Hence, the approach can easily be implemented as part of risk-based test strategy development in small and medium enterprises as well as in agile environments without specific prerequisites.

The remainder of this paper is structured as follows. Section 2 summarizes the underlying approach to risk-based test strategy development. Section 3 presents the lightweight approach to risk probability estimation. Section 4 provides an initial evaluation of the probability estimation approach. Finally, Sect. 5 concludes the paper and highlights directions of future research.

2   Background: Risk-Based Testing and Test Strategy Development

Many testing processes (e.g., [7, 8]) as well as standards (e.g., [2]) recommend the use of risk information in software testing. Several risk-based approaches for software testing have been proposed such as by Bach [9], Amland [10], and van Veenendaal [11]. Furthermore, comprehensive frameworks and guidelines for risk management as well as for risk-based testing have been developed in context of software security; prominent examples are the Risk Management Framework (RMF) [12] and the OWASP Testing Guide [13]. These approaches implement or are accompanied by various different ways for assessing risks [14–17].

In the remainder of this section we describe a previously presented, empirically evaluated process for risk-based test strategy development [18] as one example of how probability and impact values may be determined and used in practice. It is an essential first step when introducing risk-based testing in an organization [19] to establish a risk-based test strategy that anchors risk-orientation as basis for all testing activities in the entire software lifecycle. The process has been evaluated as part of a research transfer project for introducing risk-based testing in five small and medium software development companies.

In general, a *test strategy* describes how testing is organized and performed on the different test levels [20]. The usually rather generic strategy has to be refined for its implementation in context of a specific project or product iteration. The refinement results in a concrete test approach that defines the different types of testing that need to be performed, the test and quality assurance techniques to be applied, and the coverage and exit criteria used for tacking the progress and determining test completion.

Figure 1 provides an overview of the overall process for risk-based test strategy development. It consists of different steps, which are either directly related to the risk-based test strategy development (shown in bold font) or which are used to establish the preconditions (shown in normal font) for the process by linking test strategy development to the related processes (drawn with dashed lines) of defect management, requirements management and quality management.

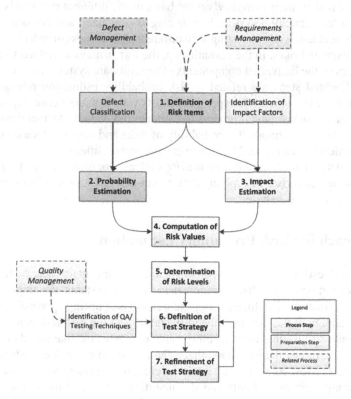

Fig. 1. Probability estimation in risk-based test strategy development [18]. The highlighted steps relate to risk probability estimation as explored in this paper.

The process for risk-based test strategy development comprises seven core steps, which are as follows. In the first step, *risk items*, which are the basic elements associated with risks and mapped to test objects, are defined. They can be derived from established structures used in defect and requirements management. In the second step, for each risk item *probability values* are estimated which express their likelihood of defectiveness. For probability estimation, one can use data from defect classification [21] that captures and enhances the relevant data obtained from defect management. In the third step, for each risk item *impact values* are estimated which express the consequences of risk items being defective [22]. As the impact is closely related to the expected value of the components for the user or customer, requirements management is a main source of data for impact estimation. In the fourth step, *risk values* are computed from the estimated probability and impact values. The computed risk values can be used to group risk items, for example, according high, medium and low risk. In the fifth step, the spectrum of risk values is partitioned into *risk levels*, which comprise a further level of aggregation. The purpose of distinguishing different risk levels is to define classes of risks such that all risk items associated to a particular class are considered equally risky and as a consequence are subject to the same intensity of quality assurance and test measures. In the sixth step, the *test strategy is defined* on the basis of the different risk levels. For each risk level the test strategy describes how testing is organized and performed. Distinguishing different levels allows testing with different rigorousness in order to adequately address the expected risks. In the seventh step, the *test strategy is refined* to match the characteristics of the individual components of the software system (i.e., risk items).

The highlighted steps are related to risk probability estimation relevant for the approach further explored in this paper. Probability estimation is a core step in the risk-based test strategy development process to estimate risk values. As mentioned before, experts seem to underestimate the probability of risks and may produce contradicting as well as misleading estimates [5]. However, risk probabilities can be estimated based on historical defect data collected from previous releases or related projects. To support also less mature enterprises in applying defect data-based risk probability estimation, a lightweight approach is required.

3   Approach for Risk Probability Estimation

To improve risk estimation in context of small and medium enterprises, we recommend combining expert opinion with quantitative data from the systems' development history [18]. Figure 1 illustrates the different steps of a risk-based testing approach. It includes, first, the estimation of the factors probability and impact for each risk item.

In the context of testing the probability value expresses the likelihood of defectiveness of a risk item, i.e., the likelihood that a fault exists in a specific module that may lead to a failure. Most companies maintain a defect management system for reporting failures, tracing failures to faults and documenting their resolution. These systems capture the defect history of a software system and can serve as basis for deriving data for estimating future risk probabilities [18].

Modeling the usually complex relationship between software faults and resulting failures [20] requires considerable effort and a consistent data set that may not be available in practice. In contrast, projects in small and medium organizations are often following an on-demand, agile approach. Our lightweight approach has been inspired by the "yesterday's weather" principle used for planning in Extreme Programming [23]. It is a simple rule used in effort estimation, e.g., for estimating the amount of work a team can complete in a sprint. Instead of a complex estimation approach the rule suggests to use the amount of work completed in the previous sprint as estimate for the next sprint. This estimate is not meant to replace human judgement but to provide a quantitative basis that can be easily adjusted by including the knowledge and experience of human decision-makers. The benefit of this rule-based approach is its simplicity and widespread applicability.

In our approach we follow the same principle. Probability estimates are derived from defect counts of the previous version. In short, components with a high defect count in the last version are estimated to be likely defective in the next version and, vice versa, components that were already free of defects in the last version are still considered to be defect-free. Estimates based on defect counts are usually mapped to probability levels (e.g., high, medium and low), which are used to construct risk matrices that are the basis for the subsequent testing activities as shown in Fig. 2.

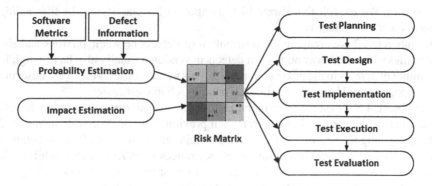

Fig. 2. Risk-based testing approach.

Extrapolation from defect counts provides a fast and easy way to estimate risk probabilities. However, the approach is based on the assumption of a continuous process and environment that keeps influence factors on risks stable over consecutive versions. Therefore, the estimates are adjusted by expert opinion to include knowledge about disruptive events in the development process, in testing or in the usage of the software system [24]. Human judgement is also used to decide about boundary cases and new components where no historical records are available.

4 Evaluation

We demonstrate the feasibility and explore the limits of the proposed lightweight estimation approach by applying it in context of the open-source project *jEdit*[1]. The tool jEdit is a widely used and mature programmer's text editor with – according to the project's description – hundreds of person-years of development behind it. It is written in Java and has been released as free software with full source code. The project jEdit has been subject to a previous study on defect prediction by Jureczko and Madeyski [25]. As part of their study the data has been made publically available and can be obtained from the *OpenScience tera-PROMISE* repository[2].

The data is used to illustrate and evaluate the approach of estimating the risk probability for source code files. In particular, we use available data in terms of defect counts per file from a "known" version n to make estimates for the next version $n + 1$. As described above, the estimates express the risk probability of a particular file containing defects according to the categories high/medium/low. A detailed analysis is provided by the following sub-sections.

- In Subsect. 4.1 we explore the distribution of defects in each individual studied version. We show that in each version there are a small number of highly defective files, a moderate number of files with a few defects, and a large number of defect-free files. We exploit this Pareto-like distribution for classifying the files as *high*, *medium* or *low* defective.

- In Subsect. 4.2 we compare the distribution of defects between versions and show that files with a high/low number of defects in version n usually also have a high/low number of defects in the next version $n + 1$. This trend is observable over consecutive versions and builds the foundation for making reliable estimates.

- In Subsect. 4.3 we estimate the high/medium/low probability of files being defective based on defect counts obtained from their previous version. We evaluate the results by computing the *accuracy* of the estimates (classification) as well as the number of *overestimates* and *underestimates*. Accuracy ranges from 73% to 78%, while critical underestimates are less than 1% and critical overestimates remain below 4%.

- In Subsect. 4.4 we discuss the threats to validity of our evaluation.

4.1 Versions and Defect Distributions

In our study we analyze four versions of jEdit (3.2.1, 4.0, 4.1, and 4.2), which are related to a continuous period of development of about three years. In this time interval the code base has steadily grown, from 129 KLOC (272 Java files) in version 3.2.1 to 171 KLOC (367 Java files) in version 4.2. In the same time the number of defects has been reduced from 382 to 106 defects (Table 1).

---

[1] http://www.jedit.org/
[2] http://openscience.us/repo/defect/ck/jedit

Table 1. Key measures of the studied versions of jEdit.

Version	LOC	Files	Defects	Avg. defects/file	Max defects/file	Defect-free files
3.2.1	128,883	272	382	1.40	45	67%
4.0	144,803	306	226	0.74	23	75%
4.1	153,087	312	217	0.70	17	75%
4.2	170,683	367	106	0.29	10	87%

In each version a Pareto-like distribution of defects to files can be observed. The top 10% of defective files contain 71% / 77% / 74% / 90% of the defects in each of the studied versions. The histograms in Fig. 3 show the distribution of files per number of defects. In each version there are a large number of defect-free files (0 defects), a moderate number of files with only a few defects (1 to 3 defects) and a small number of files with many defects (4 or more defects). In the following, we can exploit this information for classifying files as *low*, *medium* or *high* defective.

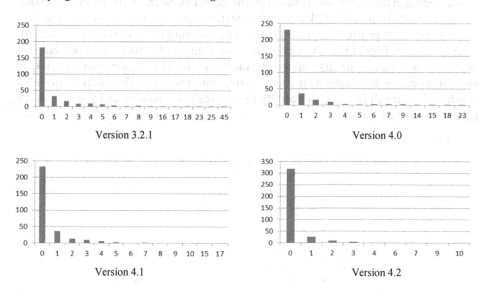

Version 3.2.1

Version 4.0

Version 4.1

Version 4.2

Fig. 3. Number of files per defect count for each version.

4.2 Defective Files in Consecutive Versions

Although the studied application is growing over time and undergoes many modifications, a large share of the files (75% to 89%) can be traced from one version to the next. These files are present in version n as well as in version $n + 1$. In this section we explore if we can take advantage of the relationship these files share over consecutive versions to make reliable estimates.

The underlying assumption is that files that have a large number of defects in one version will also have many defects in the next version and, vice versa, files that do not have any defects will stay defect-free. The overall number of defects changes over time and so does the number of defects per file. However, we are mainly interested if the overall relationship in terms of high/medium/low number of defects stays the same. We first investigate our assumption by charting the cumulative gain in terms of defects over all files in version $n + 1$ when ordering them according to their defectiveness in version n. Figures 4, 5 and 6 show the respective gain charts (lift plot [26]).

The x-axis of the gain chart depicts the number of files subject to testing. The y-axis shows the cumulative percentage of total defects that can be found in testing when a particular ordering of the files is applied. The *optimal* ordering (green curve) is what one gets when sorting the files according to their actual number of defects in version $n + 1$. It represents the best way of ordering the files for testing. However, the actual numbers are unknown at the time of testing and this ordering can only be determined from an ex-post view on the data. At the time of testing one has to rely on estimates. In the worst case such estimates are equal to guessing, which would correspond to a *random* ordering of the files (gray dotted 45-degree diagonal line). In our approach the *estimation* is based on the defect numbers of the previous version n. These numbers are already known when testing for version $n + 1$ is going to start and can therefore be used for prioritization, i.e., ordering the files (blue line) accordingly. If several files in version n have the same number of defects, their ordering for version $n + 1$ cannot be determined. Without any further information for making estimates one has to assume a random ordering for these files. The different possible combinations result in range defined by the curves *best estimate* and *worst estimate* (green/red dashed lines).

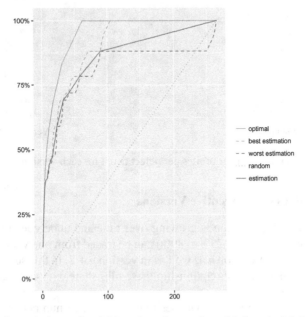

Fig. 4. Cumulative gain in version 4.0 based on the number of defects in 3.2.1. (Color figure online)

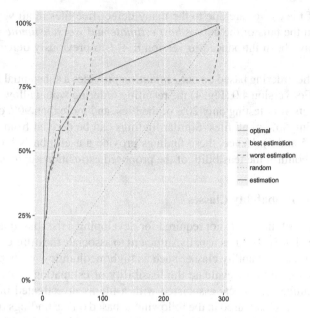

Fig. 6. Cumulative gain in version 4.2 based on the number of defects in 4.1. (Color figure online)

Concerning our assumption, we can make the following observations. First, the steep initial growth of the estimate curve shows that files with a high number of defects in version *n* are usually also containing a high number of defects in version *n + 1*. Second,

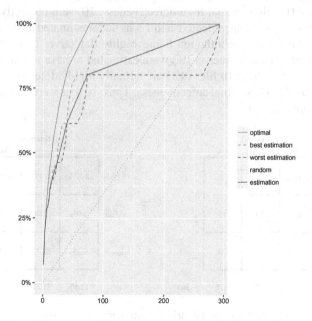

Fig. 5. Cumulative gain in version 4.1 based on the number of defects in 4.0. (Color figure online)

the long tails of the curves are due to the many defect-free files in all versions. Third, the gap between the tails of the curves *best estimate* and *worst estimate* indicates that some defects have been introduced in version *n + 1* to previously defect-free files of version *n*.

In general, the ordering based on our *estimation* provides a substantial improvement over guessing. For version 4.0 (Fig. 4) the resulting ordering would allow finding about 75% of the defects after testing only 20% of the files, and more than 90% defects can be found after testing 50% of all files. Similar findings can be derived from all three gain charts (Figs. 4, 5 and 6). Hence, these findings provide a useful basis for making estimates and they confirm the feasibility of the proposed estimation approach.

4.3 Estimating Probability Classes

An exact ordering of the files is not required for developing a risk-based test strategy as initially described in Sect. 2. It is usually sufficient to associate the different files or parts of the system to risk probability classes such as high/medium/low probability of being defective. In this section we evaluate the feasibility of estimating probability classes based on the number of defects associated with a file as investigated in the previous Sect. 4.2. The classification used in the following is based on the findings from Sect. 4.1, where we explored the defectiveness of the files per version as *high* = ≥ 4 defects, *medium* = 3 to 1 defects, *low* = 0 defects.

Figures 7, 8 and 9 show the confusion matrix that result from estimating probability classes for the three versions 4.0, 4.1 and 4.2. Estimated numbers are shown on the x-axis of the confusion matrix and actual numbers are shown on the y-axis. Thus, the matrix for version 4.0 can be read as follows. The first row shows that out of the 11 files (4%) in version 4.0 with an actual high defectiveness, 10 were correctly estimated to have a high probability of being defective and 1 was underestimated as having a medium probability of being defective although being highly defective. In contrast, the first column shows that in total 33 files (12%) were estimated to have a high probability of being defective. Out of these 10 files (4%) are actually highly defective, 13 (5%) have a medium and 10 (4%) a low actual defectiveness. Thus, 10 files were classified correctly and 23 were overestimated.

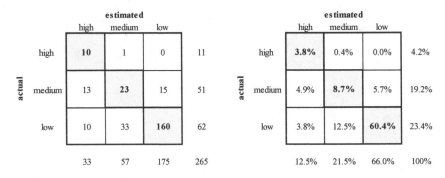

Fig. 7. Confusion matrix for estimates of version 4.0.

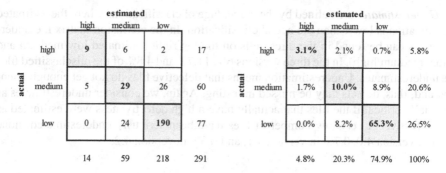

Fig. 8. Confusion matrix for estimates of version 4.1.

Fig. 9. Confusion matrix for estimates of version 4.2.

Various performance measures can be computed from the confusion matrix to evaluate the estimates. In the following we look at (1) *accuracy* as well as the number of (2) *overestimates* and (3) *underestimates*.

Accuracy is defined as the percentage of correct classifications over all classifications. In the confusion matrix the correct estimates can be found in the three diagonal cells from the top left (estimated high and actual high) to the bottom right (estimated low and actual low). The correct estimates in our study led to an accuracy of 72.8% in version 4.0, 78.4% in version 4.1, and 75.6% in version 4.2.

Overestimates are defined by the percentage of classifications where the estimated classification is higher than the actual classification. In the confusion matrix the overestimates can be found in the three cells on the lower left (estimated high/medium and actual medium/low). For the three versions 4.0, 4.1 and 4.2 the overestimates are 21.1%, 10% and 19.6%. Overestimates ("false alarms") mean that files are subject to more rigorous testing than actually considered necessary. From the perspective of a risk-based approach, overestimation may lead to a waste of time and resources. Furthermore, in terms of "false alarms" they reduce the confidence in the estimates. These problems are particularly critical for files that were estimated to have a high probability of being defective yet they were found to actually have a low defectiveness. Only a small number of critical overestimates were produced: 3.8% for version 4.0, none (0%) for version 4.1, and 2.1% for version 4.2.

Underestimates are defined by the percentage of classifications where the estimated classification is lower than the actual classification. In the confusion matrix the underestimates can be found in the three cells on the top right (estimated low/medium and actual medium/high). In the three versions 6%, 11.7% and 4.8% of the misclassified files are underestimates. Underestimation means that defective files do not get enough attention and, thus, defects may be missed in testing. Again, we consider underestimates as especially critical if the files that actually have a high defectiveness were estimated as low defective. A very low number of files have been seriously underestimated: none (0%) in version 4.0, 0.7% in version 4.1, and 0.3% in version 4.2.

4.4 Threats to Validity

The prerequisite for applying the proposed approach is a complete and consistent record of defects mapped to files for each release over an extended period of time. Reliable, high-quality defect data is also a major factor for the validity of our evaluation. We therefore selected a publically available data set that has been used in a previous, rigorously reviewed empirical study on defect prediction [25].

Defect severity has not been considered in our study. The analyzed defect data does not include severity ratings of individual defects. In our initial approach [18] we suggested using severity ratings to weight defects, which provides the possibility to adjust the ordering if several files have the same number of defects. However, for the large share of files found to be defect-free the estimation will not change. One may even decide to ignore defect severities when estimating risk probabilities as this information is included in the impact side of risk that has to be included in a next step of the risk-based testing process (which is outside the scope of this study).

The approach relies on information derived from the files in the previous version. This information is not available for new files. In our initial approach we considered all new files relevant for testing, implicitly assuming a high probability of being defective. However, in our study we found that most new files are actually defect-free and the remaining ones only have few defects. Therefore our initial assumption seems to be too pessimistic and it produces overestimates.

The discussed threats affect the validity of the evaluation, in particular, its construct and internal validity. Concerning external validity it is clear that a generalization from only one studied case is limited as in any case study research [27]. The main goal of our study was to demonstrate the feasibility of the approach, which we were able to show in the selected case. Furthermore, the studied system can be considered representative for long-running projects developing desktop applications. However, further replications are necessary to validate our findings in different contexts.

5   Conclusion and Future Work

Estimating risk probabilities is an important step in risk-based testing. However, this step is often performed in an informal way, based on expert opinion and intuition rather than on quantitative data. One of the reasons is the lack of availability of such data in projects performed in small and medium enterprises or in agile environments. These projects neither have the time nor the resources for establishing additional procedures for data collection and analysis. Similarly, sophisticated risk estimation procedures are out of scope for these projects.

In this paper we therefore proposed a lightweight approach for estimating the risk probability in risk-based software testing following the "yesterday's weather" principle. Probability estimates are based on defect numbers from the preceding version. Simplicity of the estimation approach is of foremost concern. It is intended to be easily implemented as part of risk-based test strategy development in small and medium enterprises without specific prerequisites. The only required source of information is defect data from previous versions, which can usually be derived from existing defect databases.

To investigate the feasibility of the approach we performed an evaluation on the popular open-source application jEdit. We used historical defect data to estimate the defect probability of files for three consecutive versions. Our estimates achieve an accuracy of 73% to 78%. Furthermore, they resulted in a low number of critical overestimates (less than 4%) and only a few underestimates (less than 1%). The results show that the approach is capable to satisfy the requirements suggested for applying defect prediction as basis for risk-based testing [28].

In this paper our focus was on a lightweight estimation technique with the goal to find the simplest approach that could possibly work. As part of future work we will investigate strategies to improve the estimation approach and to increase its accuracy while still keeping it simple. Our aim is to include easy-to-compute process metrics and product metrics to augment the probability estimates based on defect data.

Acknowledgments. This work has been supported by the COMET Competence Center program of the Austrian Research Promotion Agency (FFG), and the project MOBSTECO (FWF P 26194-N15) funded by the Austrian Science Fund.

References

1. Felderer, M., Schieferdecker, I.: A taxonomy of risk-based testing. Int. J. Softw. Tools Technol. Transf. **16**(5), 559–568 (2014)
2. ISO/IEC/IEEE 29119-2:2013 Software and systems engineering – Software testing – Part 2: Test processes. International Organization for Standardization, Geneva (2013)
3. Felderer, M., Ramler, R.: A multiple case study on risk-based testing in industry. Int. J. Softw. Tools Technol. Transf. **16**(5), 609–625 (2014)
4. Felderer, M., Ramler, R.: Risk orientation in software testing processes of small and medium enterprises: an exploratory and comparative study. Software Qual. J. **24**(3), 519–548 (2016)
5. Ramler, R., Felderer, M.: Experiences from an initial study on risk probability estimation based on expert opinion. In: Joint Conference of the 23rd International Workshop on Software Measurement and the Eighth International Conference on Software Process and Product Measurement (IWSM-MENSURA), pp. 93–97. IEEE (2013)
6. Beck, K.: Extreme Programming Explained: Embrace Change. Addison-Wesley, Boston (2000)

7. Spillner, A., Rossner, T., Winter, M., Linz, T.: Software Testing Practice: Test Management: A Study Guide for the Certified Tester Exam ISTQB Advanced Level. Rocky Nook, Santa Barbara (2007)
8. Black, R.: Advanced Software Testing. Guide to the ISTQB Advanced Certification as an Advanced Test Manager, vol. 2. Rocky Nook, Santa Barbara (2009)
9. Bach, J.: James Bach on risk-based testing: how to conduct heuristic risk analysis. Softw. Test. Qual. Eng. (STQE) Mag., 23–28, November/December 1999
10. Amland, S.: Risk-based testing: risk analysis fundamentals and metrics for software testing including a financial application case study. J. Syst. Softw. **53**(3), 287–295 (2000). Elsevier
11. van Veenendaal, E.: The PRISMA Approach. Uitgeverij Tutein Nolthenius, The Netherlands (2012)
12. CERT: Risk Management Framework (RMF). United States Computer Emergency Readiness Team, US-CERT, July 2013
13. OWASP: Testing Guide Ver. 4, Open Web Application Security Project, September 2014
14. Kontio, J.: Risk management in software development: a technology overview and the Riskit method. In: 21st International Conference on Software Engineering. ACM (1999)
15. Felderer, M., Haisjackl, C., Pekar, V., Breu, R.: A risk assessment framework for software testing. In: Margaria, T., Steffen, B. (eds.) ISoLA 2014. LNCS, vol. 8803, pp. 292–308. Springer, Heidelberg (2014). doi:10.1007/978-3-662-45231-8_21
16. Herrmann, A.: The quantitative estimation of IT-related risk probabilities. Risk Anal. **33**(8), 1510–1531 (2013)
17. Vose, D.: Risk Analysis: A Quantitative Guide. Wiley, Hoboken (2008)
18. Ramler, R., Felderer, M.: A process for risk-based test strategy development and its industrial evaluation. In: Abrahamsson, P., Corral, L., Oivo, M., Russo, B. (eds.) PROFES 2015. LNCS, vol. 9459, pp. 355–371. Springer, Cham (2015). doi:10.1007/978-3-319-26844-6_26
19. Felderer, M., Ramler, R.: Integrating risk-based testing in industrial test processes. Software Qual. J. **22**(3), 543–575 (2014)
20. ISTQB: Standard glossary of terms used in software testing. Version 2.1 (2010)
21. Felderer, M., Beer, A.: Using defect taxonomies for testing requirements. IEEE Softw. **32**(3), 94–101 (2015)
22. Gitzel, R., Krug, S., Brhel, M.: Towards a software failure cost impact model for the customer: an analysis of an open source product. In: 6th International Conference on Predictive Models in Software Engineering (PROMISE). ACM (2010)
23. Beck, K., Fowler, M.: Planning Extreme Programming. Addison-Wesley Professional, Boston (2001)
24. Felderer, M., Haisjackl, C., Breu, R., Motz, J.: Integrating manual and automatic risk assessment for risk-based testing. In: Biffl, S., Winkler, D., Bergsmann, J. (eds.) SWQD 2012. LNBIP, vol. 94, pp. 159–180. Springer, Heidelberg (2012). doi:10.1007/978-3-642-27213-4_11
25. Jureczko, M., Madeyski, L.: Towards identifying software project clusters with regard to defect prediction. In: 6th International Conference on Predictive Models in Software Engineering (PROMISE). ACM (2010)
26. Witten, I.H., Eibe, F.: Data Mining: Practical Machine Learning Tools and Techniques. Morgan Kaufmann, San Francisco (2005)
27. Runeson, P., Höst, M., Rainer, A., Regnell, B.: Case Study Research in Software Engineering: Guidelines and Examples. Wiley, Hoboken (2012)
28. Ramler, R., Felderer, M.: Requirements for integrating defect prediction and risk-based testing. In: 42nd Euromicro Conference on Software Engineering and Advanced Applications. IEEE (2016)

Gaining Certainty About Uncertainty

Testing Cyber-Physical Systems in the Presence of Uncertainties at the Application Level

Martin A. Schneider[✉], Marc-Florian Wendland, and Leon Bornemann

Fraunhofer FOKUS, Berlin, Germany
martin.schneider@fokus.fraunhofer.de

Abstract. A cyber-physical system (CPS) comprises several connected, embedded systems and is additionally equipped with sensors and actuators. Thus, CPSs can communicate with their cyber environment and measure and interact with their physical environment. Due to the complexity of their operational environment, assumptions the manufacturer have made may not hold in operation. During an unforeseen environmental situation, a CPS may expose behavior that negatively impactsits reliability. This may arise due to insufficiently considered environmental conditions during the design of a CPS, or – even worse – it is impossible to anticipate such conditions. In the U-Test project, we are developing a configurable search-based testing framework that exploits information from functional testing and from declarative descriptions of uncertainties. Itaims at revealing unintended behavior in the presence of uncertainties. This framework enables testing for different scenarios of uncertainty and thus, allows to achieve a certain coverage of those, and to find unknown uncertainty scenarios.

Keywords: Cyber-Physical systems · Reliability · Search-based testing · Uncertainty · UML state machines

1 Introduction

Cyber-physical systems (CPS) are increasingly affecting our daily lives, e.g. in form of an autopilot of airplanes and autonomous cars, medical devices such as insulin pumps, or less visible in logistic centers that are receiving, storing and distributing goods. They often perform safety-critical tasks (as for autonomous vehicles and medical devices) or mission-critical tasks (as for logistic centers). Due to this criticality and their impact on our daily lives, it is even more important that CPSs work reliably, otherwise health or business is at risk.

Due to their nature, CPS interact with their cyber environment as well as with their physical environment. Along with the increasing connectivity and pervasiveness of

The research leading to these results has also received funding from the European Union's Horizon 2020 Programme under grant agreement no. 645463.

© Springer International Publishing AG 2017
J. Großmann et al. (Eds.): RISK 2016, LNCS 10224, pp. 129–142, 2017.
DOI: 10.1007/978-3-319-57858-3_10

CPSs, the complexity of such interaction increases as well and is getting more complex, in particular for the physical world. Manufacturers cannot predict all circumstances, in particular with respect to the physical world, CPSs are exposed to. They have to make assumptions to make the design and development of CPSs manageable and affordable. Incomplete knowledge leads to uncertainties about their assumptions. If such an assumption fails while a CPSs is in operation, it may heavily impact its reliability and may harm human beings in their environment. Hence, finding uncertainties and testing CPSs in their presence is inevitable to increase their reliability. Since the complexity of the environment and the uncertainties of manufacturers' assumptions are difficult to grasp, traditional testing approaches are not sufficient and have to be adapted to overcome these issues.

In this paper, we propose a search-based approach to testing CPSs that copes with the challenges of the complexity of the environment and the implicit uncertainties of manufacturers' assumptions. The proposed approach provides means to declaratively describe uncertainties that are already known, e.g.due to analysis or from field tests. These descriptions are then used to bootstrap the search-based algorithm, to confine the search space and to find new uncertainties. The presented approach is subject to ongoing work done under the European research project U-Test[1].

The remaining paper is organized as follows: Sect. 2 discusses related work relevant for this paper, Sect. 3 introduces the uncertainty taxonomy used as a conceptual model for declarative description of uncertainties with respect to CPSs and catches a glimpse on declarative descriptions of uncertainties by means of an uncertainty taxonomy. Section 4 describes the proposed methodology for uncertainty testing of CPS. Section 5 closes with a conclusion and future work.

2   Related Work

2.1   Uncertainty

The term uncertainty has several meanings in different sciences and contexts as pointed out by Ramirez et al. [1]. While we are not specifically interested in the meaning in the science of psychology and economics and can ignore them, even in the field of systems engineering this term has different meanings with respect to latent or unknown properties and behaviors of a software system [2] or from the perspective of assumptions upon a certain goal [3].

However, a recognized article from Walker et al. [4] defines uncertainty as "any deviation from the unachievable ideal of completely deterministic knowledge of the relevant system". This definition takes into account the fact that there might be different kinds of knowledge beside completely deterministic knowledge. Ramirez et al. [1] defines uncertainty from the perspective of a dynamically adaptive system as a system state of incomplete or inconsistent knowledge such that it cannot decided which environmental or system configuration holds.

---

[1] http://www.u-test.eu.

Refsgaard et al. [5] specify incomplete, inaccurate, unreliable, inconclusive, or potentially false information sources for uncertainty. Ramirez et al. [1] collected several sources of uncertainties from the literature, e.g. missing or ambiguous requirements, false assumptions, unpredictable entities or phenomena in the execution environment, incomplete or inconsistent information caused by imprecise, inaccurate, and unreliable sensors. Thus, uncertainties can be introduced in the requirements, design, and runtime phase.

Walker [4] also introduces the classification in epistemic and variability uncertainties and called this the nature of an uncertainty: epistemic uncertainty results from missing knowledge whereas variability uncertainty results from the variability, for instance in human and natural systems, and is also called aleatory, stochastic, or ontological uncertainty. Erkoyuncu et al. [6] and Refsgaard et al. [5] also use the terms epistemic uncertainty and stochastic or aleatoric uncertainty in order to express the unpredictability of an event.

According to the classification of nature of uncertainties from Walker [4], Erkoyuncu et al. [6] describe the characteristics of epistemic uncertainties by a lack of knowledge. Further research may increase the amount of knowledge and thus, reduce epistemic uncertainty. In contrast, aleatoric uncertainties are characterized to be stochastic and random where the uncertainty cannot be reduced by further research.

In order to determine the knowledge level about an uncertainty, Walker [4] introduced a scale reaching from statistical uncertainty to total ignorance: *Statistical uncertainty* can be described in statistical terms. *Scenario uncertainty* is characterized by scenarios that indicate what might happen in the future, and what the effects to the system are. *Recognized ignorance* means that functional relationships are nearly unknown and there is no significant scientific basis for developing acceptable scenarios. However, for

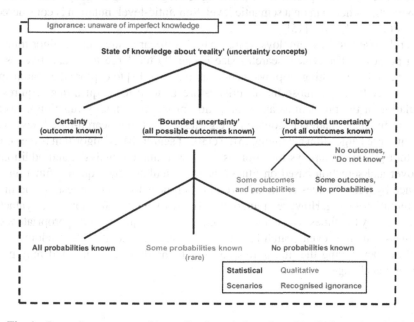

Fig. 1. Brown's taxonomy of imperfect knowledge adapted by Refsgaard et al. [5]

reducible uncertainties, this missing knowledge can be investigated in order to shift such recognized ignorance to scenario uncertainty or even statistical uncertainty. *Total ignorance* comprises all the uncertainties that one is aware of but have no or only little knowledge, those we do not know, in principle as well as those uncertainties we are not aware of.

Refsgaard [5] merged Walker's knowledge level with Brown's [7] spectrum of confidence by a taxonomy of imperfect knowledge as shown in Fig. 1. This taxonomy distinguishes uncertainties by the knowledge of possible outcomes and the probabilities of the different outcomes. Refsgaard [5] mapped this taxonomy to Walker's scale described above.

However, as discussed by Erkoyuncu [6], there are also opinions that uncertainties do not have a probability assigned and this is the main distinction between uncertainties and risks[8, 9]. Uncertainty is considered as a source of risk [10]. Erkoyuncu [6] distinguishes uncertainty from risk by the lack of any outcome predictability – in contrast to Walker and Refsgaard – and that uncertainty covers positive outcomes while risk only covers negative outcomes.

2.2   Mutation Testing, Fault-Based Test Generation and Search-Based Testing

Mutation testing [11] and mutation analysis [12] are techniques to introduce faults either in the implementation, i.e. source code, or in the specification, e.g. models, to assess the quality of test cases and test suites. Mutation operators are considered as fault models that are applied to code or models and can be used to generate test cases [13, 14]. Higher order mutation testing uses combinations of mutation operators to find real bugs [15]. Mutation operators are specific to a modelling or programming language and thus, work on a syntactic rather than on a semantic level. Semantic-level mutation is considered as a relevant research-topic [15].

Search-based testing employs search-based software engineering algorithms for testing purposes. The typical search-space is usually too large for exhaustive testing. Thus, search-based testing employs metaheuristics [16, 17] to explore the search space more efficiently. Since those metaheuristics are generic techniques that requires the formulation of the problem as an optimization problem, a quality function is used to assess individual candidate solutions, e.g. test cases for search-based testing. A frequently used algorithm belonging to the class of search-based algorithm is the genetic algorithm [18] that employs mutation as used by mutation analysis, and additionally crossover and selection based on fitness values calculated by a quality function. The guidance by fitness values is one of several differences to mutation testing and higher order mutation testing. However, mutation and crossover is usually done on a syntactical level guided by the fitness calculation. Depending on the quality and appropriateness of the fitness function, even search-based testing may degenerate into random testing. Therefore, developing the fitness function has to be done carefully and may pose a significant challenge.

3 The Uncertainty Taxonomy: Declarative Descriptions of Uncertainty

In this paper, we consider uncertainties coming from the environment and accordingly, call them environmental uncertainties [19–23]. According to Cheng [20], environmental uncertainties come from the physical environment and the cyber environment. Uncertainties from the physical environment come from unforeseen or environmental conditions with a lack of knowledge about it and may also result from sensor failures or noisy environments [23]. Uncertainties from the cyber environment may result from malicious threats or unexpected (human) input [23].

In addition to environmental uncertainties, uncertainties of CPS may also occur within the technical infrastructure when connected embedded systems, sensors and actuators interact in an unforeseen way or errors occur in the communication infrastructure of a CPS. However, in this paper we consider uncertainties in the environment of a CPS since uncertainties in the infrastructure are different compared to environmental level uncertainties, are often originating from technical uncertainties within the CPS's technical infrastructure and have to deal with other aspects than the environment, e.g. elasticity and virtualization. Therefore, we assume the infrastructure was sufficiently tested and is working fine.

Environmental uncertainties may impact the application running on the technical infrastructure of a CPS either directly, if the application is confronted with invalid or unexpected data or behavior, e.g. from another system or a user, or indirectly because a sensor works correctly but its reading is tampered by physical circumstances such as smoke. Therefore, we refer to environmental uncertainties by the term *application level uncertainties*.

An application level uncertainty is constituted by a circumstance that does not comply with the specified or expected environmental behavior, and may not be foreseen by a CPS' manufacturer. If a CPS behaves in an undesired manner due to an uncertainty, i.e. in a way that negatively impacts its reliability, we call such a behavior an *uncertain behavior* to indicate that it results from an unforeseen or unexpected environmental condition. We distinguish between *known uncertain behaviors* that are known by analysis or field tests, i.e. before the system is deployed, and those that are not known a priori, and call them *unknown uncertain behaviors*. Accordingly, the corresponding uncertainties are referred to by the terms *known uncertainty* for those that may be known a priori and *unknown uncertainty* for uncertainties one not aware of.

To describe known uncertainties, we developed a taxonomy that allows to specify their characteristics. The purpose of the taxonomy is twofold. On one hand, by providing a scheme for properties of uncertainties may support their analysis and thus, their understanding. Furthermore, we use it to test for these, in order to find uncertainty scenarios and even new uncertainties as explained in Sect. 4.

The characteristics of uncertainties comprise properties such as the origin, i.e. whether the uncertainty occurs in the physical or the cyber environment, or its causes, on a high-level distinguishing between human behavior, natural process and technological process. Figure 2 provides an excerpt of the taxonomy.

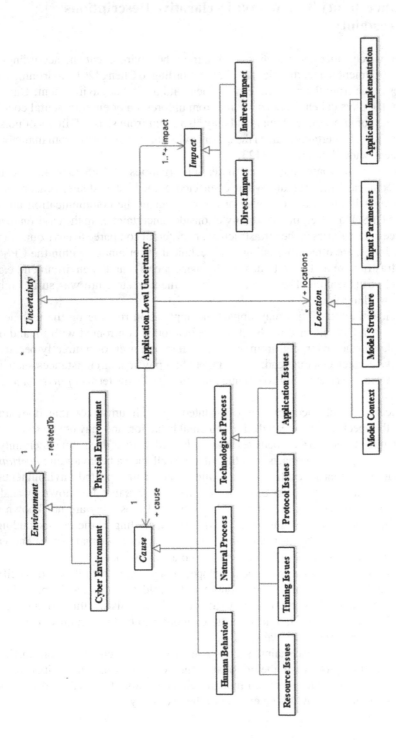

Fig. 2. Excerpt of the taxonomy for application level uncertainties

We aim at characterizing uncertainties systematically by its *origin*, its *cause*, its *location* and its *impact* on a system. The origin is related to the *environment* where the uncertainty may occur. This is denoted by the environment and may either be the *cyber environment* or the *physical environment*. The *cause* is used to characterize the originator of an uncertainty. We basically distinguish human behavior, natural process and technological processes as cause for an uncertainty. A person that regularly interacts with a cyber-physical system may show behavior that may contribute to an uncertainty. Natural processes are usually related to the physical environment where randomness may come into play, a very simple example may be radiation that may impact the readings of a sensor. Technological processes are distinguished in those related to resources, timing, protocols and the application itself.

Timing issues may result from the uncertainty whether a system is working with the expected performance while abstracting of real time, e.g. by a cycle counter.

Resource issues are reflecting different issues with respect to the cyber world as well as to the real world, e.g. resource competition meaning that two instances are working on or using the same resources and thus interfering with each other. *Resource location* means that the expected resource is not where it is expected to be. *Insufficient resources* comprises uncertainties regarding the demanded and the provided resources where the demanded resources are higher than the provided resources, e.g. a missing resource item in the physical environment or insufficient CPU resources with respect to the cyber environment.

Protocol issues summarize different uncertainties with respect to communication protocols. *Interoperability issues* occur if the specification of a communication protocol is ambiguous and two communication partners differ in their protocol implementation *Faulty protocol implementation* is a result of an incorrect protocol implementation leading to communication errors between two communication partners, e.g. different components of the application or between the application and the infrastructure of the cyber-physical system.

Application issues comprise uncertainties inherent to the application itself. Communication issues with platform is referring to situations where the application fails to communicate with platform devices, maybe resulting from a faulty application configuration. Functional faults are traditional implementation bugs within the application.

The concept *impact* represents the impact of an uncertainty from the environment to the impacted element of a cyber-physical system, such as hardware and/or application.

4 Uncertainty Testing

This section introduces the proposed approach for search-based uncertainty testing by (i) providing an overview how to create models suitable for uncertainty testing in the first subsection and (ii) describing how the proposed approach evolve such models, aiming at revealing uncertain behavior by eventual test case generation and execution, in the second subsection. Since we employ a genetic algorithm, we require a quality function that provides a measure to evaluate whether we are about to find uncertain behavior of a system under test (SUT). To do so, we provide a model-based framework to describe relevant behavioral characteristics of the SUT for fitness evaluation in the third subsection. The last subsection provides information that can be used to describe an exit criterion when to stop uncertainty testing in terms of coverage criteria (Fig. 3).

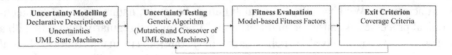

Fig. 3. Overview of uncertainty testing process steps

4.1 Modelling for Uncertainty Testing

Modelling for uncertainty testing requires two artifacts: modelled uncertainties and functional models in terms of UML state machines. The latter one can be easily obtained from a functional testing process performed in a model-based way. Such models can be reused for uncertainty testing and thus, reducing the effort to start the proposed approach. If functional descriptions in form of UML state machines do not exist, they can be created by anyone who has enough information on the requirement but does not need specific knowledge about uncertainties. The more challenging task is to describe characteristics of uncertainties. Such information can be obtained by a risk analysis approach or by obtaining information from tests in the field. Figure 4 provides an example of a UML state machine describing valid interaction of the environment with the SUT. It describes a simple geo-locating system that determines the positions of tags whose positions are determined through a set of locators. The locators receive the signal of a tag and the application calculates its position via triangulation. First, tags are configured for the system (transition 'configureTag') and locators mounted (transition 'subsequentMonitoring'). After that, the system is calibrated (transition 'calibrate'), and by changing the position of a tag (transition 'setPosition'), it can be checked whether the tag's position is correctly calculated by the system (transition 'getAllPositions').

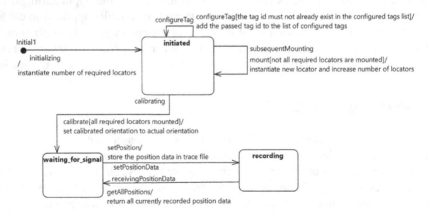

Fig. 4. UML state machine providing a functional description

The system may not calculate a tag's position correctly if a locator is mounted after the system has been calibrated. The corresponding uncertainty would influence the correct recording of position data. The uncertainty consists in the unmodified position of the locators, i.e. that locators are not remounted after calibration. Hence, the correct functionality may be discontinued by an application level uncertainty related to the *mount* operation on an already mounted locator (referred by the transition 'subsequent-Mounting') after the system has been calibrated. Figure 5 provides a description of such an uncertainty whose impact refers to this *mount* operation.

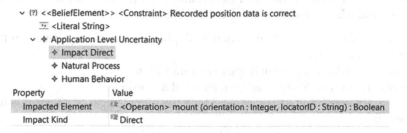

Fig. 5. Example of a modelled application level uncertainty

For this small example, it's enough information to perform uncertainty testing as described in the next subsection.

4.2 Evolving UML State Machines and Generating Test Cases

Uncertainties at the application level comprise all the stimuli from the environment of the SUT. The purpose of uncertainty testing is (i) discovering *known uncertain behaviors* resulting from uncertainties that may be known at design time, and (ii) discovering *unknown uncertain behaviors* that may occur in the presence of yet unknown uncertainties.

Since we do not know all the manifestations of an uncertainty and would like to reveal unknown uncertain behavior resulting from unknown uncertainties, we employ search-based techniques to efficiently walk through the input space. Aiming at measuring whether we are approaching an uncertainty that may expose known or unknown uncertain behavior or if we have already discovered one, we exploit different outputs of the SUT as inputs to a fitness function.

The modelled uncertainties and the functional models as described in the previous subsection form the basis for evolving state machines. Thus, we exploit the coupling effect [24]. The goal is to gain state machines of which at least one path reveals uncertain behavior.

Mutation. Mutation is performed on one hand using information from modelled uncertainties, and on the other hand independent from that by using information of the system provided by the test model. In contrast to mutation analysis and search-based testing, we take into account semantical information provided by modelled uncertainties for mutation and eventual test generation. Thus, we do not apply mutation on a syntactical level but on the semantic level as well. By this approach, we can reduce the search space further.

We apply mutations to transitions based on information from modelled uncertainties, evaluating its *impact* property that refers to a single operation or an interface containing operations. Several mutations of the same element are allowed, although a few combinations of mutations are excluded to generate executable test cases eventually, e.g. those combinations that do not lead to a new state machine, e.g. in case one mutation is the inverse of another mutation. Based on the literature [9, 18], we use the mutation operators as follows and adapted them to UML state machines.

- *Add Transition*: Adds a new transition by duplicating an existing one and setting a new source and target state.
- *Remove Transition*: Completely removes a transition.
- *Reverse Transition*: Swap source and target of a transition.
- *Change Source/Target of Transition*: Move the source/target of a transition to any other state.
- *Remove Trigger of Transition*: Transforms a transition to a completion transition.
- *Change Trigger of Transition*: Changes the operation of a transition's trigger to another one of the same interface.

Based on the example state machine depicted in Fig. 4 and an application level uncertainty depicted in Fig. 5, we can identify those transitions that refer to the operation *mount* as the uncertainty. Such a mutation looks as in Fig. 6.

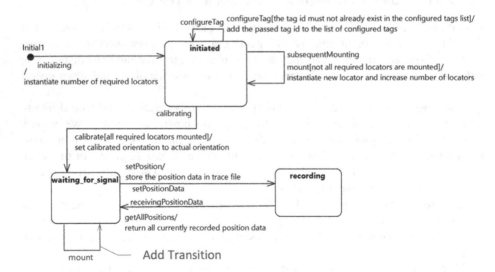

Fig. 6. UML state machine mutated by adding a transition with trigger *mount*

Crossover. Mutations are the atomic piece of information to perform uncertainty testing. Therefore, for the recombination/crossover of state machines, we solely consider mutations instead of whole state machines. We propose to use the following crossover operators: *Combine all mutations of both parents.* This yield one new child UML state machine. *Uniform crossover:* swap *n* mutations of both state machines. This yield two new child state machines. This approach can be refined by swapping an unfit mutation of state machine A with a fit mutation of state machine B if the share at least one path. *Combine only the fittest path(s):* This yields one new state machine with less mutations.

Test Case Generation. We generate test cases based on evolved UML state machines using Microsoft's Spec Explorer [30] that calculates all paths through it. To generate executable test cases, we use UML-based behavioral description of so-called execution invariants that describe those sequences that all test cases must respect. A simple example of such an execution invariant is that a system must be switched on before it can be configured. These execution invariants are different from system requirements since we would like to intentionally violate system requirements. Execution invariants represent those invariants whose violation is actually impossible and would lead to test cases that could not be executed against the system under test or that would impede evaluation of test cases.

Considering again the example state machine depicted in Fig. 4. It has two transitions named 'setPosition' to change the position of a tag and 'getAllPositions' to retrieve the position calculated by the SUT. Each time we change the position, we would require to retrieve the calculated position to decide whether it still matches sufficiently. Therefore, we would describe this as an execution invariant in form of a sequence diagram as shown in Fig. 7.

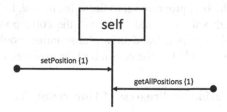

Fig. 7. Simple example of an execution invariant requiring that *getAllPositions* is called immediately after *setPosition*

4.3 Modelling Fitness Factors

To specify use-case specific factors, we provide stereotypes to identify elements that allow obtaining values from test runs (*FitnessFactorProviders*) that may be compared with an expected value by the corresponding counterpart (*ExplicitProvider*). These can be used for instance, to measure the distance between a measured position and the actual position. For measured values without any comparative value, *ImplicitProviders* can refer to them. An optional threshold can be specified together with a *metricGoal* that specifies whether the actual, measured value should be minimized, maximized or approach the threshold. In case of *ExplicitProviders*, the difference between the actual and the expected value can be minimized or maximized. System-specific factors can be identified by the same means. Furthermore, we use generic measures such as response time, CPU load, and memory consumption if we can obtain these values from the SUT. Figure 8 shows the different stereotypes for fitness factor descriptions.

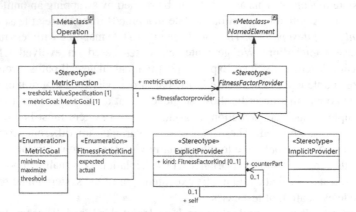

Fig. 8. Framework for model-based fitness factors description

With respect to the example given in Fig. 4, we would use the stereotype *Explicit-Provider* referring to the operation to retrieve the position that was actually set with the *kind* property set to the value *expected* to describe the expected position data, i.e. *setPosition*, and a second one referring to the operation that retrieves the position data calculated by the SUT with the *kind* property set to the value *actual*, i.e. the operation *getAllPositionData*. Since both values should be equal, the corresponding *MetricFunction* would have the *metricGoalminimize*, and an implementation would calculate the difference between the values provided by the *actual* and the *expected* fitness factor provider.

4.4 Metrics for Measuring the Progress of Uncertainty Testing

To measure the progress of uncertainty testing and to be able to provide an exit criterion to determine when the testing process should be stopped, we described an Uncertainty Space Coverage metric that would be first step towards this goal.

It measures all generations of evolved state machines related to a single uncertainty. The Uncertainty Space is spanned by all the possible mutation on triggers, guards and effect of transition in a UML state machine denoted by the variable N. If g is the number of steps of evolving a state machine, i.e. the number of generations (equal to the number of mutations), we can describe all the possible mutations by

$$NG(N, g) = \frac{g(g + 1)}{2}N - 2\sum_{j=1}^{g} \sum_{k=1}^{j} (k - 1)$$

that can be simplified to the following version:

$$NG(N, g) = \frac{g(g + 1)}{2} N - 2 \sum_{j=1}^{g} \frac{j(j + 1)}{2} - j$$

The Uncertainty Space comprises all possible combinations:

$$UncertaintySpace(N, g) = \sum_{j=1}^{g} NG(N, g)$$

As expected, the uncertainty space may grow strongly with the number of mutations applied to a single state machine and strongly depends on the constant N.

5 Conclusion and Future Work

We introduced an approach for testing the reliability of CPS in the presence of uncertainty with the help of declarative descriptions and UML state machines evolved by a genetic algorithm. The approach aims at finding manifestations of known uncertainties and unknown uncertainties and the corresponding uncertain behaviors. We described execution invariants to ensure generation of executable test cases. Finally, we proposed a coverage criterion based on the uncertainty space appropriate for specifying an exit criterion for uncertainty testing.

Since this paper presents ongoing work, there is still a lot of work to do. Obviously, information used from uncertainty description is currently. For an effective approach, other kind of information should be obtained, particularly with respect to the cause of an uncertainty. Currently, the number of mutation operators is limited. Krenn et al. [11] provides an exhaustive specification of mutation operators for UML state machines. Since the uncertainty space is very huge, more ways to confine the process should be investigated. Eventually, the approach has to show its feasibility, effectiveness and efficiency by a thorough evaluation and compare it with traditional approaches.

References

1. Ramirez, A.J., Jensen, A.C., Cheng, B.H.C.: A taxonomy of uncertainty for dynamically adaptive systems. In: Proceedings of the 7th International Symposium on Software Engineering for Adaptive and Self-managing Systems, Piscataway, NJ, USA, pp. 99–108 (2012)
2. Goldsby, H.J., Cheng, B.H.C.: Automatically discovering properties that specify the latent behavior of UML models. In: Petriu, D.C., Rouquette, N., Haugen, Ø. (eds.) Model Driven Engineering Languages and Systems, pp. 316–330. Springer, Berlin Heidelberg (2010)
3. Welsh, K., Sawyer, P.: Understanding the scope of uncertainty in dynamically adaptive systems. In: Wieringa, R., Persson, A. (eds.) Requirements Engineering: Foundation for Software Quality, pp. 2–16. Springer, Berlin Heidelberg (2010)
4. Walker, W.E., et al.: Defining uncertainty: a conceptual basis for uncertainty management in model-based decision support. Integr. Assess. 4(1), 5–17 (2003)

5. Refsgaard, J.C., van der Sluijs, J.P., Højberg, A.L., Vanrolleghem, P.A.: Uncertainty in the environmental modelling process – a framework and guidance. Environ. Model Softw. **22**(11), 1543–1556 (2007)
6. Erkoyuncu, J.A., Roy, R., Shehab, E., Cheruvu, K.: Understanding service uncertainties in industrial product–service system cost estimation. Int. J. Adv. Manuf. Technol. **52**(9–12), 1223–1238 (2011)
7. Brown, J.D.: Knowledge, uncertainty and physical geography: towards the development of methodologies for questioning belief. Trans. Inst. Br. Geogr. **29**(3), 367–381 (2004)
8. Faro, D., Rottenstreich, Y.: Affect, empathy, and regressive mispredictions of others' preferences under risk. Manag. Sci. **52**(4), 529–541 (2006)
9. Knight, F.H.: Risk, Uncertainty and Profit. Courier Corporation (2012)
10. Emblemsvåg, J.: Life-Cycle Costing: Using Activity-Based Costing and Monte Carlo Methods to Manage Future Costs and Risks. Wiley, New Jersey (2003)
11. Krenn, W., Schlick, R., Tiran, S., Aichernig, B., Jobstl, E., Brandl, H.: MoMut::UML model-based mutation testing for UML. In: 2015 IEEE 8th International Conference on Software Testing, Verification and Validation (ICST), pp. 1–8 (2015)
12. Fabbri, S.P.F., Delamaro, M.E., Maldonado, J.C., Masiero, P.C.: Mutation analysis testing for finite state machines. In: Proceedings of 5th International Symposium on Software Reliability Engineering, pp. 220–229 (1994)
13. DeMillo, R.A., Lipton, R.J., Sayward, F.G.: Program mutation: a new approach to program testing. Infotech State Art Rep. Softw. Test. **2**, 107–126 (1979)
14. Ammann, P.E., Black, P.E., Majurski, W.: Using model checking to generate tests from specifications. In: Proceedings Second International Conference on Formal Engineering Methods (Cat.No.98EX241), pp. 46–54 (1998)
15. Jia, Y., Harman, M.: An analysis and survey of the development of mutation testing. IEEE Trans. Softw. Eng. **37**(5), 649–678 (2011)
16. Luke, S.: Essentials of metaheuristics (2013). lulu.com
17. McMinn, P.: Search-based software test data generation: a survey: research articles. Softw. Test Verif. Reliab. **14**(2), 105–156 (2004)
18. Harman, M., Zhang, Y., Mansouri, S.A.: Search based software engineering: a comprehensive analysis and review of trends techniques and applications. King's College (2009)
19. Cheng, B.H.C., Sawyer, P., Bencomo, N., Whittle, J.: A goal-based modeling approach to develop requirements of an adaptive system with environmental uncertainty. In: Schürr, A., Selic, B. (eds.) Model Driven Engineering Languages and Systems, pp. 468–483. Springer, Berlin Heidelberg (2009)
20. Tackling Uncertainty for Transportation Cyber-Physical Systems | CPS-VO. http://cps-vo.org/node/11229. Accessed 25 Sep 2016
21. NIST Foundations for Innovation for Cyber-Physical Systems. http://events.energetics.com/NIST-CPSWorkshop/. Accessed 25 Sep 2016
22. Ramirez, A.J., Jensen, A.C., Cheng, B.H.C., Knoester, D.B.: Automatically exploring how uncertainty impacts behavior of dynamically adaptive systems. In: Proceedings of the 2011 26th IEEE/ACM International Conference on Automated Software Engineering, Washington, DC, USA, pp. 568–571 (2011)
23. Whittle, J., Sawyer, P., Bencomo, N., Cheng, B.H.C., Bruel, J.-M.: RELAX: a language to address uncertainty in self-adaptive systems requirement. Requir. Eng. **15**(2), 177–196 (2010)
24. DeMillo, R.A., Lipton, R.J., Sayward, F.G.: Hints on test data selection: help for the practicing programmer. Computer **11**(4), 34–41 (1978)

Risk Management During Software Development: Results of a Survey in Software Houses from Germany, Austria and Switzerland

Michael Felderer[1]([✉]), Florian Auer[1], and Johannes Bergsmann[2]

[1] Institute of Computer Science, University of Innsbruck, Innsbruck, Austria
{michael.felderer,florian.auer}@uibk.ac.at
[2] Software Quality Lab GmbH, Linz, Austria
johannes.bergsmann@software-quality-lab.com

Abstract. Resource constraints during development require an elaborated decision-making process supported by risk information. The goal of this paper is to investigate the state-of-practice of risk management during development in software houses. For this purpose, we conducted a survey in Germany, Austria, and Switzerland where 57 software houses participated. The survey results are triangulated by results from literature and interviews with a subset of the survey participants. Results from the survey show that less than a third of the companies performs risk management during development. Main reasons for not performing risk management are lack of resources, need and knowledge. An important application area of risk assessment results is the prioritization of test cases. Finally, technical product risks as well as project risks are commonly applied risk assessment criteria.

1 Introduction

Developing software systems or services within budget and schedule requires an elaborated decision-making process supported by risk information [1,2]. For instance, competent decisions on what to release [3,4] or on how much to test [5,6] are supported by risk management activities. Given the importance of risk management during software development, it is important to investigate its state-of-practice and to provide respective guidelines. This holds especially for software houses, i.e., companies whose primary products are software, for which risk management during development is essential to guarantee quality and to deliver within time and budget. The goal of this paper is to investigate the state-of-practice of risk management during development in software houses. For this purpose, we present results of a survey conducted by the University of Innsbruck together with the Austrian consultancy company Software Quality Lab in software houses from Germany (D), Austria (A) and Switzerland (CH), the so called "DACH region". Overall 57 software houses from the DACH region responded to questions on risk management during software development. The results were complemented by interviews and results from related surveys.

© Springer International Publishing AG 2017
J. Großmann et al. (Eds.): RISK 2016, LNCS 10224, pp. 143–155, 2017.
DOI: 10.1007/978-3-319-57858-3_11

The results presented in this paper provide information on the state-of-practice and are equally relevant for research (by guiding it to relevant topics) and practice (by serving as a baseline for comparison). The presented survey on risk management was part of a comprehensive survey with additional questions in the areas of process models, release planning, requirements engineering, implementation, and testing [7].

This paper is structured as follows. Section 2 presents related work. Section 3 discusses the survey goal, design and execution. Section 4 presents results and discusses them. Finally, Sect. 5 concludes the paper.

2   Background and Related Work

In this section, we provide background on risk management and summarize related results on risk management during development from other surveys reporting respective results. Relevant related results reported in these studies address the project effort spent on implementation, tool support during implementation as well as the usage of agile practices during implementation. In the following paragraphs we summarize these quantitative and qualitative results and later in Sect. 4 we relate them to our findings.

A *risk* is the chance of injury, damage or loss and is typically determined by the combination of the probability of an event and its consequence [8]. Amongst others, risks can refer to the software project or product level. For instance, with regards to project risks, the Project Management Body of Knowledge (PMBOK) [9] defines risk as an uncertain event or condition that, if it occurs, has a positive or negative effect on a project's objectives. With regards to product risks, the IEEE 829:2008 standard on software and system test documentation [10] defines risk as the combination of the probability of an abnormal event or failure and the consequence(s) of that event or failure to a system's components, operators, users, or environment.

Risk management is according to the standard ISO/IEC/IEEE 24765:2010 on systems and software engineering [11] an organized process for identifying and handling risk factors to identify what might cause harm or loss (identify risks); to assess and quantify the identified risks; and to develop and, if needed, implement an appropriate approach to prevent or handle causes of risk that could result in significant harm or loss. Reasons to apply risk management are to increase the likelihood and impact of positive events, and decrease the likelihood and impact of negative events in the project [9]. According to Sommerville [12] risk management is one of the most important jobs for a project manager.

A *risk management process* contains the core activities *risk identification, risk analysis, risk treatment* and *risk monitoring* [13]. In the risk identification phase the risk items are identified. In the risk analysis phase the probability and impact of risk items and, hence, the risk exposure is estimated. On the basis of risk exposure values, risk items may be prioritized and assigned to risk levels. This results in a risk classification. In the risk treatment phase the actions for obtaining a satisfactory situation are determined and implemented. In the risk monitoring phase the risks are tracked over time and their status is reported. In addition, the effect of the implemented actions is determined. The activities risk identification and risk analysis are often collectively referred to as *risk assessment*, while the activities risk treatment and risk monitoring are referred to as *risk control*.

The factors that influence how a risk is assessed are called risk criteria and can be quite diverse including associated cost and benefits, legal and statutory requirements, socio-economic and environmental aspects, the concerns of stakeholders, priorities and other inputs to the assessment [8].

Several surveys address risk management during development [14–16]. Haberl et al. [15] asked in 2011 for the reasons to not applying risk analysis. 32.3% of all respondents answered to not apply it because of missing methodological skills, 24.5% mentioned insufficient resources as a reason, 17.4% did not see the necessity and finally 10.8% argued to not have the time for it. The remaining 15% mentioned other reasons that were not further discussed in the report. Similar issues for risk management integration were also observed by Kajko-Mattsson et al. [14] in 18 of the 37 surveyed companies (48%). Amongst others, the following three reasons (similar to [15]) were found. First, that employees do not see necessity for risk management, which may make it more difficult to motivate necessary work for risk assessment. Second, another reason are inexperienced risk managers that do not have enough knowledge and experience in risk management. Third, risk management requires to allocate resources exclusively to the task. This may be a problem for organizations. In the case of insufficient resources for risk management, risks cannot adequately be monitored and controlled. As a consequence, risk management possible fails. Overall, one can state that according to available studies, missing methodological knowledge, insufficient resources and a lack of time are very common reasons to not apply risk management.

Kajko-Mattsson et al. [14] found in 2008 that risk management in the context of software development is essential and that its integration into the process of development is important. Furthermore, the authors concluded that the implementation of risk management is experienced to be very difficult in the studied organizations [14]. Nevertheless, Haberl et al. [15] noted that almost 70% of participants stated that they perform risk management in their projects. A similar percentage was found in 2014 by Arnuphaptrairong [16] for the investigated software companies from Thailand. 77.5% of them responded to have risk management integrated in their software development process. In addition, Arnuphaptrairong asked the participants which techniques for risk identification are practiced. The most common answers were brain storming (73.3% of all respondents), check lists (70%) and interview (23.3%). Other techniques like top ten lists, risk dimensions or the delphi method, were only mentioned by at most 16% of the participants to be used in practice. Concerning risk roles, 80.6% of all participants identified the project manager as the person responsible for software project risk management.

3   Survey Goal, Design, Distribution, and Analysis

This section provides the survey goal and research questions (Sect. 3.1), the survey design (Sect. 3.2), the survey distribution (Sect. 3.3), as well as the survey analysis (Sect. 3.4). Finally, Sect. 3.5 provides a summarizing timeline of the performed survey design, distribution and analysis activities.

3.1   Goal and Research Questions

The goal of this survey is to investigate the role of risk management during development in software houses from Germany, Austria and Switzerland. The target audience of the survey are therefore software houses that are located in Germany, Austria or Switzerland and do not operate in a domain that may impose restrictions on their software development, e.g., medical or automotive. Based on the goal and taking industrial relevance from experiences of the involved company Software Quality Lab into account, we investigate the following three research questions (RQs):

RQ 1. How common is risk management during development and what are the reasons for not performing risk management?

RQ 2. For what purposes are risk assessment results applied for?

RQ 3. Which risk assessment criteria are considered for risk management during development?

3.2   Survey Design

In this section, we present the sampling plan, the questionnaire design and the performed pilot test. As the presented survey on risk management was performed as part of a more comprehensive survey, the presentation of the survey design is based on a previous publication [7]. The survey design is based on lessons learned and guidelines reported by other researchers in software engineering [17,18].

Sampling Plan. The sampling plan describes how the participants are representatively selected from the target population. The first decision, whether a probabilistic, non-probabilistic or census sample should be considered, was already made by selecting the target audience. Given that no list of all companies exists that have the characteristics of to target audience, a truly probabilistic or census sample is not feasible. The first (probabilistic) would require an enumeration of all members of the target audience to select randomly participants and the later (census) can as well only be conducted if all individuals of the target audience are known. As a result, non-probabilistic sampling was chosen.

As a method to draw the sample from the population quota sampling with the two strata geographical location of the software house (Germany, Austria or Switzerland) and number of employees (less or equal 10, 11 to 100 and more than 100) was applied.

Overall 57 software houses, 19 from each of the three countries, evenly distributed over the three company sizes were selected and could be consulted within the given time and resources. Based on the activities relevant for software houses from the OECD [19] industry categories, i.e., 62 – Computer programming, consultancy and related activities, as well as 631 – Data processing, hosting and related activities; web portals, the overall number of software houses in Germany, Austria and Switzerland could be estimated based on data from governmental statistical offices. For Germany, the "IKT-BRANCHE IN DEUTSCHLAND" [20] report identified 61,029 companies in 2013 that are classified with one of the two categories[1]. For Austria, the governmental statistical office reported 13,281 companies in the respective categories[2] in 2012. Finally for Switzerland, the federal statistical office measured 2008 in the census of companies[3] 15,466 companies that have amongst their main activities programming, information technology consulting and data processing. As a result, the total number of software houses in the DACH region can be estimated with 90,000 $(61,029 + 15,466 + 13,281 = 89,776)$. Taking the population size of 90,000 into account, with the 57 participating companies a precision [17], which measures how close an estimate (resulting from the survey data) is to the actual characteristic in the population, of 87% is achieved.

Questionnaire Design. The questionnaire was designed based on the experiences of Software Quality Lab and the involved researchers in conducting surveys as well as academic findings of related surveys (see Sect. 2) and the software engineering body of knowledge (SWEBOK) [21]. The knowledge and practical consultancy experience of Software Quality Lab was a valuable input to design the questionnaire. Furthermore, a technical report of a survey on software quality conducted by Winter et al. [22] in 2011 provided many useful insights for the questionnaire design. The questions included in the questionnaire were transformed into closed-ended questions and ordered by topic. The questionnaire was implemented and performed online with the survey tool LimeSurvey[4]. Each research question was addressed by one question in the questionnaire, which was embedded into a larger questionnaire on software quality processes. The answer options for each questions are shown in Figs. 2, 3, and 4. The complete questionnaire is available via the first author upon request.

Pilot Test. The questionnaire was validated *internally*, i.e., by the involved researchers and Software Quality Lab, as well as *externally* by six employees of software houses. Internally, there were several iterations and the involvement of researchers and industrialists guaranteed a high quality review from different perspectives. Externally, the reviewers provided valuable, written feedback to further improve the questionnaire.

---

[1] http://bit.ly/1Sqfb3z.
[2] http://bit.ly/22IjjeS.
[3] http://bit.ly/22IkScL.
[4] http://www.limesurvey.org.

3.3 Survey Distribution

The distribution of the questionnaires among the potential participants included a pre-notification, the invitation with the questionnaire, reminders and a thank-you letter. The survey distribution started on April 1, 2015. The participants were selected by using Google Maps and searching for 'software company'. Searching for this term reveals all software companies at the related location. Furthermore, information about the number of employees for each identified software house were determined. This made it possible to come up with 450 participants – 50 small, 50 medium and 50 large software houses per country. Two weeks after the pre-notification emails were sent, the invitation emails with a link to the online survey were distributed. As a result, 13 participants responded to not wish to participate and 20 software houses participated. One reminder was sent in the middle of the survey (end of April 2015) to remember possible participants about the survey. Due to the low number of responses, additional 500 software companies were contacted via email. In addition, new participants were searched and contacted exclusively by phone to invite them to the survey. During three days within the last week, 200 potential software houses in Germany, Austria and Switzerland were called and asked for participation. In this three days 18 software houses could be convinced to participate. Thus, the response rate for the phone calls was 9%, which is double the response rate of the email invitations (4% for the first half of the survey and 3% for the second). During the phone calls, also some of the reasons against the participation were mentioned. Amongst others, no time, no interest, already having participated in similar surveys as well as the absence of the respective decision maker were mentioned. The survey distribution ended on May 22, 2015.

3.4 Survey Analysis

The data was first analyzed *quantitatively* and then *qualitatively* by interviews with survey participants and evidence extracted from related work.

As the responses for each question were nominally scaled, the votes for each question were counted and then visualized in bar charts. In addition, we performed 12 interviews with survey participants (i.e., 21% of all participants) to triangulate the quantitative analysis and to identify the reasons behind some survey answers. The semi-structured interview type was chosen, because the structured interview limits the discussion freedom to enter unforeseen subtopics or ask questions that may arise during the interview. Another alternative would have been the unstructured interview. However, this form would have not allowed to ask prepared questions of interest that emerged during the analysis of the empirical survey. Telephone calls were used contact each participant in an economic and for the interviewee time- and place-flexible way. In the short interview one question on implementation was asked. In addition, the non-structured part of the interview followed subtopics of interest that were raised by the interviewee or that turned out as a result of previously conducted interviews to be of interest.

3.5 Survey Timeline

This section summarizes the survey design, distribution and analysis by providing the concrete timeline in which the respective activities were performed in 2015. Figure 1 shows the timeline for survey design, distribution and analysis activities. Activities with concrete dates in parentheses were performed in the given date range, the other activities were performed during the whole month.

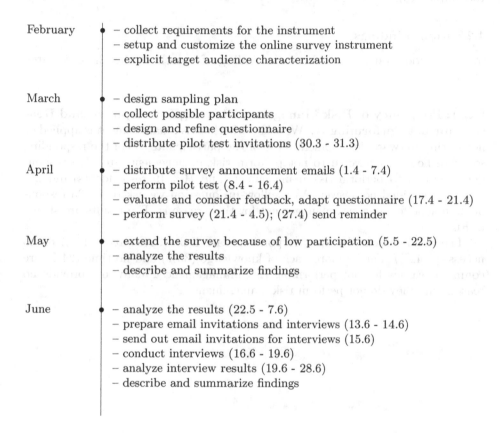

February
- collect requirements for the instrument
- setup and customize the online survey instrument
- explicit target audience characterization

March
- design sampling plan
- collect possible participants
- design and refine questionnaire
- distribute pilot test invitations (30.3 - 31.3)

April
- distribute survey announcement emails (1.4 - 7.4)
- perform pilot test (8.4 - 16.4)
- evaluate and consider feedback, adapt questionnaire (17.4 - 21.4)
- perform survey (21.4 - 4.5); (27.4) send reminder

May
- extend the survey because of low participation (5.5 - 22.5)
- analyze the results
- describe and summarize findings

June
- analyze the results (22.5 - 7.6)
- prepare email invitations and interviews (13.6 - 14.6)
- send out email invitations for interviews (15.6)
- conduct interviews (16.6 - 19.6)
- analyze interview results (19.6 - 28.6)
- describe and summarize findings

Fig. 1. Timeline of the survey

4 Results and Discussion

In this section, we first present the demographics of our survey, then we present and discuss main findings for each of the three research questions, and finally we discuss threats to validity.

4.1 Demographics

Overall 57 software houses, 19 from Germany, 19 from Austria and 19 from Switzerland, participated in the survey. Most of the software houses (84%) stated that they perform more than one type of software project. On average three types were stated. The three most common project types are development of web-applications (71%), individual software (61%), and standard software (56%).

In the sample of 57 software houses small, medium and large companies are present with a similar frequency: 38% of the companies are small-sized (up to 10 employees), 35% medium-sized (11 to 100) and 26% large-sized (more than 100 employees).

4.2 Main Findings

In this section we present the main findings for each of the three research questions.

RQ 1: Frequency of Risk Management During Development and Reasons for not Performing It. We asked whether risk management is applied or not during software development. 58% of the participants (33 of the responding software houses) answered to not perform risk management, 26% (15 respondents) stated to perform risk management, and 16% (9 respondents) did not know or provided no answer. As a follow-up question we asked the 33 respondents not performing risk management for their reasons. The results are shown in Fig. 2.

The main reasons for most respondents are lack of resources (48%) or no necessity (42%). Furthermore, lack of knowledge (33%) and no time (24%) are common reasons for not performing risk management. Finally, 6% provide no reason why they do not perform risk management.

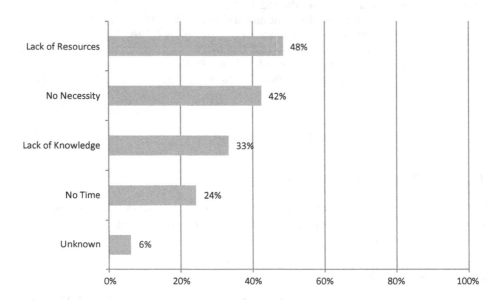

Fig. 2. Reasons for not performing risk management (N = 33)

In two surveys from 2014 [16] and 2011 [15] it was found that at least two of three projects apply risk management. However, according to the collected survey data of this study only about every third company performs risk management. Thus, it may seem that the number of risk management practitioners decreased. However, it should be considered that the survey presented in this paper had a well-defined target audience consisting of software houses in the DACH region, whereas Haberl et al. did not restrict their target audience. Thus, it may be that because of the inclusion of other industry branches (more mission or safety-critical domains like finance or production) the ratio of companies that perform risk management that also influences software development is higher. The higher rate reported in Arnuphaptrairong [16] could be due to regional differences.

Haberl et al. [15] and Kajko et al. [14] identified missing methodological knowledge, insufficient resources and a lack of time as the most common reasons to not apply risk analysis. The reasons for not performing risk management reported in our survey, i.e., lack of resources, lack of knowledge as well as no time are similar.

Also a subset of 12 respondents was interviewed whether they applied risk management or not and how this influenced their software projects. Reasons mentioned during the interviews for not applying risk management are that the interviewees were not convinced by the idea of it or that they had the feeling that it does not fit for agile development. Interviewees that declared to use risk management highlighted to use it because it helps them to assess the priorities of the requirements, it stresses the importance of specific tests and helps to decide which requirements should be included in the next release.

RQ 2: Application of Risk Assessment Results. Figure 3 shows the application areas of risk assessment results as provided by the 15 respondents who perform risk management. 73% of them apply risk assessment results to prioritize test cases. 53% apply them to target test selection methods, to allocate resources, and to define test criteria, respectively. Furthermore, 33% apply them to evaluate remaining risks in test reports. Finally, 13% of the respondents who perform risk management do not name an application area of risk assessment results.

In terms of the usage of the risk management and its affect on the software project, the survey found that the main application of risk management is to prioritize test cases. Similar, the participants mentioned during the interviews that again the main usage is to prioritize the requirements. Furthermore, they claimed that it is used to stress certain tests or to decide which requirements should be part of the next release. The main application of risk management is to prioritize activities, especially during software testing. Prioritization of test cases is an important application of risk assessments in software testing [23–25].

Interviewees that declared to use risk management pointed out during the interviews to use risk management because it helps them to assess the priorities of the requirements and to use this information for test and release management. Furthermore, the importance of risk management for specific tests was highlighted.

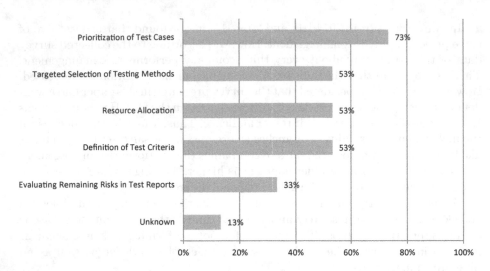

Fig. 3. Application areas of risk assessment results (N = 15)

RQ 3: Risk Assessment Criteria Considered for Risk Management.
Figure 4 shows the risk assessment criteria considered during risk management as reported by the 15 respondents who perform risk management. 93% of them consider technical product risk (i.e., a technical risk directly related to a system, service or test object), and project risk (i.e., risks related to management and control of a (test) project), respectively. 67% consider business product risk (i.e., a business risk directly related to a system, service or test object), 60% criticality (which informally integrates other risk assessment criteria), and 27% frequency of execution. Finally, 7% of the respondents who perform risk management do not which risk assessment criteria are considered during risk management.

In the survey of Arnuphaptrairong [16] from 2014 the participants stated that brain storming, check lists and interview are common methods for risk identification. Furthermore, most participants identified the project manager as the person responsible for software project risk management. Although neither this result nor results from other surveys provide results on the actual usage of risk assessment criteria as our survey does, we can assume from Arnuphaptrairong [16] that assessment criteria are often not specified explicitly (as brain storming plays an important role) or that project risks play an important role (as project managers are often responsible for risk management).

4.3   Threats to Validity

In this section we discuss the main threats to validity of the presented study and measures performed to mitigate them. First, the survey was answered by representatives from 57 software houses (from overall about 90,000 software houses in the whole DACH region). Although the number of participating software houses

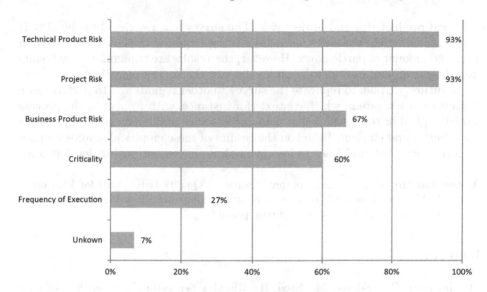

Fig. 4. Risk assessment criteria considered during risk management (N = 15)

is relatively small, the precision of the conducted survey is already 87%. Furthermore, the results were triangulated by interviews and a comparison to results of related studies. The partial deviation of the study results from those of similar studies, especially with regards to the frequency of risk management during software development in software houses, suggest that the presented results are specific for software houses and not generalizable to arbitrary domains. The questionnaire itself was reviewed internally by the involved researchers and the involved company Software Quality Lab as well as externally by six employees of software houses. Furthermore, other already validated and successfully implemented related questionnaires like [22] were taken into account when constructing the performed questionnaire. Finally, the questions asked on risk management were part of a more comprehensive survey on software quality and processes in software houses. This might reduce the threat that the survey participants have in general a positively biased attitude towards risk management in software development.

5 Conclusion

This paper presented a survey on risk management during development in software houses from Germany, Austria and Switzerland. Overall 57 software houses participated. Results from the survey show that risk management is often not performed during software development. The most important reasons for not performing risk management are lack of resources or missing necessity for it. The most important application area for risk assessment results is the prioritization of tasks like testing. The most important risk assessment criteria are technical product risk and project risk. The survey was restricted to the DACH region including the countries Germany, Austria and Switzerland, and based on a limited amount of participants. However, the results are triangulated by results from literature and interviews with a subset of the survey participants.

In future, we plan to replicate the survey in other regions and to perform case studies to investigate in which context (for instance, with respect to the process model applied or the development domain) specific risk management approaches are effective and efficient. Based on the results of these empirical studies we plan to derive practical guidelines to improve risk management during development.

Acknowledgments. The authors thank Software Quality Lab GmbH for joint operation of this survey as well as all participating companies, interview partners and colleagues who helped to make this survey possible.

References

1. Haisjackl, C., Felderer, M., Breu, R.: Riscal-a risk estimation tool for software engineering purposes. In: 2013 39th Euromicro Conference on Software Engineering and Advanced Applications, pp. 292–299. IEEE (2013)
2. Karolak, D.W., Karolak, N.: Software Engineering Risk Management: A Just-in-Time Approach. IEEE Computer Society Press, Los Alamitos (1995)
3. Felderer, M., Beer, A., Ho, J., Ruhe, G.: Industrial evaluation of the impact of quality-driven release planning. In: Proceedings of the 8th ACM/IEEE International Symposium on Empirical Software Engineering and Measurement, p. 62. ACM (2014)
4. Ruhe, G.: Product Release Planning: Methods Tools and Applications. Auerbach Publications, Boca Raton (2011)
5. Felderer, M., Schieferdecker, I.: A taxonomy of risk-based testing. Int. J. Softw. Tools Technol. Transf. **16**(5), 559–568 (2014)
6. Amland, S.: Risk-based testing: risk analysis fundamentals and metrics for software testing including a financial application case study. J. Syst. Softw. **53**(3), 287–295 (2000)
7. Felderer, M., Auer, F.: Software quality assurance during implementation: results of a survey in software houses from Germany, Austria and Switzerland. In: Winkler, D., Biffl, S., Bergsmann, J. (eds.) SWQD 2017. LNBIP, vol. 269, pp. 87–102. Springer, Cham (2017). doi:10.1007/978-3-319-49421-0_7
8. ISO/IEC: ISO/IEC 16085:2006, standard for software engineering - software life cycle processes - risk management. Std ISO IEC 16085–2006, pp. 1–46, December 2006
9. Project Management Institute: A Guide to the Project Management Body of Knowledge: PMBOK(R) Guide. Project Management Institute (2013)
10. IEEE: IEEE standard for software and system test documentation. IEEE Std 829–2008, pp. 1–150, July 2008
11. ISO/IEC/IEEE: ISO/IEC/IEEE 24765:2010 - systems and software engineering - vocabulary, p. 418 (2010)
12. Sommerville, I.: Software Engineering. International Computer Science Series. Addison-Wesley, Boston (2007)
13. ISO: ISO 31000 - risk management (2009)

14. Kajko-Mattsson, M., Nyfjord, J.: State of software risk management practice. Int. J. Comput. Sci. **35**(4), 451–462 (2008)
15. Haberl, P., Spillner, A., Vosseberg, K., Winter, M.: Survey 2011: software test in practice (2011). http://www.istqb.org/documents/Survey_GTB.pdf
16. Arnuphaptrairong, T.: Software risk management practice: evidence from Thai software firms. In: Proceedings of the International Multi Conference of Engineers and Computer Scientists, vol. 2 (2014)
17. Kasunic, M.: Designing an effective survey. Technical report, DTIC Document (2005)
18. Linaker, J., Sulaman, S.M., Maiani de Mello, R., Höst, M., Runeson, P.: Guidelines for conducting surveys in software engineering v. 1.0 (2015)
19. Working Party on Indicators for the Information Society: Information economy - sector definitions based on the internet standard industry classification (isic 4). DSTI/ICCP/IIS(2006) 2/FINAL (2007)
20. Bundesamt, S.: Ikt-branche in deutschland - bericht zur wirtschaftlichen entwicklung - ausgabe 2013 (2013). https://www.destatis.de
21. IEEE: Guide to the Software Engineering Body of Knowledge (SWEBOK): Version 3.0. IEEE Computer Society Press (2014)
22. Winter, M., Vosseberg, K., Spillner, A., Haberl, P.: Softwaretest-umfrage 2011-erkenntnisziele, durchführung und ergebnisse. In: Software Engineering, pp. 157–168 (2012)
23. Felderer, M., Ramler, R.: A multiple case study on risk-based testing in industry. Int. J. Softw. Tools Technol. Transf. **16**(5), 609–625 (2014)
24. Felderer, M., Ramler, R.: Risk orientation in software testing processes of small and medium enterprises: an exploratory and comparative study. Software Qual. J. **24**, 1–30 (2015)
25. Ramler, R., Felderer, M.: A process for risk-based test strategy development and its industrial evaluation. In: Abrahamsson, P., Corral, L., Oivo, M., Russo, B. (eds.) PROFES 2015. LNCS, vol. 9459, pp. 355–371. Springer, Cham (2015). doi:10.1007/978-3-319-26844-6_26

Author Index

Printed in the United States
By Bookmasters